5 INGREDIENTS
slow cooker

PUBLISHED IN 2019 BY BAUER MEDIA BOOKS, AUSTRALIA.
BAUER MEDIA BOOKS IS A DIVISION OF BAUER MEDIA PTY LTD.

Bauer Media Group

CHIEF EXECUTIVE OFFICER
PAUL DYKZEUL

CHIEF FINANCIAL OFFICER
ANDREW STEDWELL

Bauer Media Books

PUBLISHER
SALLY EAGLE

EDITORIAL & FOOD DIRECTOR
SOPHIA YOUNG

CREATIVE DIRECTOR
HANNAH BLACKMORE

MANAGING EDITOR
STEPHANIE KISTNER

SENIOR DESIGNER
JEANNEL CUNANAN

SENIOR EDITOR
CHANTAL GIBBS

FOOD EDITORS
SOPHIA YOUNG, KATHLEEN DAVIS

OPERATIONS MANAGER
DAVID SCOTTO

PHOTOGRAPHER
JOHN PAUL URIZAR

STYLIST
KATE BROWN

PHOTOCHEFS
ANGELA DEVLIN, NADIA FONOFF, REBECCA LYALL

RECIPE DEVELOPERS
NADIA FONOFF, ANGELA DEVLIN, ELIZABETH MACRI,
REBECCA LYALL, ELIZABETH FIDUCIA,
WARREN MENDES

ADDITIONAL TEXT
LEANNE KITCHEN

PRINTED IN CHINA
BY 1010 PRINTING INTERNATIONAL

A CATALOGUE RECORD FOR THIS
BOOK IS AVAILABLE FROM THE
NATIONAL LIBRARY OF AUSTRALIA.
ISBN 978-1-92569-540-3

PUBLISHED BY BAUER MEDIA BOOKS,
A DIVISION OF BAUER MEDIA PTY LTD,
54 PARK ST, SYDNEY; GPO BOX 4088,
SYDNEY, NSW 2001, AUSTRALIA
PH +61 2 9282 8685; FAX +61 2 9126 3702
WWW.AWWCOOKBOOKS.COM.AU

INTERNATIONAL RIGHTS MANAGER
SIMONE AQUILINA
SAQUILINA@BAUER-MEDIA.COM.AU
PH +61 2 8268 6278

ORDER BOOKS
PHONE 136 116 (WITHIN AUSTRALIA)

OR ORDER ONLINE AT
WWW.AWWCOOKBOOKS.COM.AU

SEND RECIPE ENQUIRIES TO
RECIPEENQUIRIES@BAUER-MEDIA.COM.AU

**TRUSTED BRANDS USED
IN OUR TEST KITCHEN**

THE AUSTRALIAN
Women's Weekly

5 INGREDIENTS
slow cooker

BEFORE YOU START *Slow cookers are available in a range of shapes and sizes and come with a variety of features. The recipes in this book were generally tested in different brand, shaped and sized slow cookers, including 3-litre (12-cup), 5-litre (20-cup) and 5-litre (20-cup) slow cookers. If you have a smaller or larger slow cooker, you may need to decrease or increase the ingredients in the recipe. While the ingredients for recipes using diced meat and smaller meat cuts, such as chicken wings or lamb chops, should fit in most commonly available slow cookers, larger pieces, such as whole chickens or lamb legs, were tested in the size specified in the recipe. The first step when using your slow cooker is to read the manufacturer's instructions, as each cooker will differ depending on its features. They will also outline appropriate safety measures, such as not leaving the appliance unattended at any time.*

Contents

why five?

Maximum flavour, minimum fuss –
who isn't a fan of this approach
to getting food on the table?

With just five ingredients, plus basic staples, we've created recipes that show how less can often be so much more. Bringing a slow cooker into the equation creates the perfect scenario for saving time, while building the biggest flavours.

And if slow cooking with just very few ingredients sounds like an impossible idea, it's not. We went back to the drawing board in our Test Kitchen to develop recipes using no more than five ingredients, working hard to make them not just convenient for you but delicious too. Certainly, you need to provide a few basics, but these are standard pantry items and are the types of things you're unlikely to run out of. Butter, oils, vinegars and salt and pepper: we've kept it to these simple items.

Developing the recipes, we took cues from international cuisines – Greek, Middle Eastern and Italian to Mexican, Chinese and Indian – to ensure there were plenty of varied flavours to keep everybody happy. We worked on recipes for broths, bakes, braises and biryani – and everything in between; we even went the sweet route. Yes, in your slow cooker you can make delicious desserts; check out our five-ingredient pudding, cobbler, pie, brownie and cheesecake recipes – who knew?

At their heart, the recipes in this book are structured around quality ingredients and fresh, seasonal produce, with nothing included that's esoteric or hard to source. To keep ingredient lists strictly to five, we began the development of each dish by choosing a single hero ingredient, then allowed ourselves no more than four supporting ones. We gave great thought to what those remaining ingredients should be; when forced to cook using fewer elements, we found we really questioned the value of each one. Was it absolutely right? Was there a better one to use? Did it really bring maximum flavour and goodness to the table? Anything that didn't satisfy our strict criteria, and result in the best possible outcomes, did not make the grade.

We realised too that clever use of convenience ingredients, all available from the supermarket, can be a good way to go with this easy style of cooking. Not every product that's 'convenience'

While all the recipes are designed for everyday dining, there's plenty to suit casual entertaining too. With the spectacular results you'll achieve, you'll find it hard to believe how pared back these dishes really are. Throughout the book we give Make It Six suggestions, giving you the option of adding a single additional ingredient to embellish and take things up a notch. If you've forgotten an ingredient or there's something listed that you don't really like, our Swap It tips are a useful guide to suitable substitutes.

Finally, a note on slow cookers. The technology around these has really advanced since the early days of the original Crock Pot. Newer multi-cookers perform various functions, allowing you to, among other things, sear meat and brown vegetables. Some have heatproof inners that you can put directly on the stovetop to start cooking, then transfer to the slow cooker to complete the dish.

Bringing a slow cooker into the equation creates the perfect scenario for saving time, while building the biggest flavours.

necessarily means a compromise; sometimes, when you're busy, it's smart to take a shortcut or two. Creamed canned corn, canned tomatoes, beans and chickpeas, frozen vegetables, tomato passata, caramelised onions, chutneys, curry pastes, marinades, peanut butter and bottled fruit – these types of pantry items can be kitchen lifesavers. Used well, they enhance a dish, as well as saving buckets of your precious time.

While these are versatile functions, they're not vital to have for the recipes in this book.

fridge basics

Less is more when it comes to fridge supplies. Rather than hoarding, use our suggestions here for flavour-building ingredients for your slow cooker dishes; these will take up less room in the fridge, allowing more room for perishable foods.

1
SAUCES & CONDIMENTS
Chilli sauces, miso (white and red), red curry paste, tahini, soy sauces, indian spice pastes and mustards are the basis for marinades and curries.

2
PICKLES & PRESERVES
Ingredients preserved in salt, brine, vinegar and oil, such as black and green olives, capers, kimchi, sauerkraut and preserved lemons, add interest in both flavour and texture.

3
CITRUS
Lemons, limes, oranges and mandarins can all be used for their rind, flesh and juice to add freshness. Kaffir lime leaves give a fragrant touch.

4
VEGETABLES
Celery, fennel, carrots, chillies and alliums, such as leeks, are the ideal flavour base for casseroles and stews.

5
HERBS & AROMATICS
Buy ginger and lemon grass, and woody herbs like rosemary and thyme for longevity.

pantry basics

Keeping these in your pantry means you have the flavour-boosting basis for many of our slow cooker recipes, with only a few extra ingredients needed to transform these staples into delicious, satisfying meals.

1
VINEGARS & OILS
Whether you have two or 10 different oils and vinegars in your pantry, they add flavour to your cooking.

2
SPICES & SEASONINGS
Add spices and spice mixes to breathe life into savoury and sweet recipes, for flavour, colour and complexity.

3
GRAINS, NOODLES & PASTA
Wheat and egg pastas in myriad shapes. Coloured rices and ready-cooked sachets. Dried beans, lentils, quinoa and barley are protein rich.

4
CANNED FOODS
Must-haves are canned tomatoes, beans, lentils, and coconut milk and cream, all of which will form the base for so many dishes.

5
NUTS & SEEDS
Nutrient-dense, these are great for adding texture as well as flavour. Freeze in bags for long-term storage.

Under 6 hours

spanish lentils with chorizo & prawns

PREP TIME 20 MINUTES **COOK TIME** 4 HOURS 10 MINUTES **SERVES** 4

FIVE INGREDIENTS

1 bunch fresh coriander (cilantro)

4 cured chorizo (500g)

1½ cups (300g) dried French-style green lentils

1kg (2lb) arrabbiata pasta sauce

12 uncooked large king prawns (shrimp) (900g)

STAPLES

sea salt flakes

freshly ground black pepper

extra virgin olive oil

1 Preheat slow cooker on HIGH.

2 Wash coriander; separate roots, stems and leaves. Finely chop coriander roots and stems; reserve leaves for serving. Cut chorizo into thick slices on the diagonal. Rinse and drain lentils.

3 Place chopped coriander, chorizo, lentils, pasta sauce and 3 cups (750ml) water in slow cooker; season well. Cook, covered, for 4 hours.

4 Meanwhile, peel and devein prawns, leaving tails intact. Refrigerate, covered, until required. Season prawns; stir into lentil mixture in slow cooker. Cook, covered, for a further 5 minutes or until prawns are just cooked through.

5 Drizzle stew with oil; season with pepper. Top with reserved coriander leaves; serve.

MAKE IT SIX *Add a coarsely chopped onion at the start of step 3.*

SERVE IT *with the grilled sourdough on page 130 and the simple green salad on page 106, if you like.*

chicken pho

PREP TIME 15 MINUTES **COOK TIME** 5 HOURS 30 MINUTES **SERVES** 4

FIVE INGREDIENTS

1 bunch fresh coriander (cilantro)

8 chicken drumsticks (1.2kg)

2 teaspoons chinese five spice

⅓ cup (80ml) fish sauce

200g (6½oz) dried rice stick noodles

STAPLES

2 teaspoons vegetable oil

6 black peppercorns

freshly ground black pepper

1 Wash coriander; separate roots, stems and leaves. Finely chop coriander roots and stems; reserve leaves for serving.

2 Preheat a 5-litre (20-cup) slow cooker on 'sear' (HIGH) setting.

3 Add oil and half the chicken drumsticks to slow cooker; cook uncovered, turning, for 7 minutes or until well browned. Transfer to a tray. Repeat with remaining chicken. Add chopped coriander, five spice and browned chicken to slow cooker; stir to mix.

4 Add 1.75 litres (7 cups) water, fish sauce and peppercorns to slow cooker. Adjust setting to LOW; cook, covered, for 5 hours or until chicken is tender. Transfer chicken to a large tray.

5 Strain chicken broth through a fine sieve over a large bowl; discard solids. Remove chicken meat from bones; discard skin and bones. Return strained broth and chicken meat to cleaned slow cooker. Adjust setting to HIGH; cook, covered, for a further 15 minutes or until hot. Season broth with extra fish sauce, if needed.

6 Meanwhile, place noodles in a medium heatproof bowl; cover with boiling water. Stand for 15 minutes; drain.

7 Divide noodles and chicken among bowls; ladle broth over chicken. Season with pepper and top with reserved coriander leaves; serve.

MAKE IT SIX *Add lime wedges or bean sprouts to serve.*

STORE IT *Prepare to the end of step 5 and refrigerate in an airtight container for up to 2 days, or freeze for up to 1 month. Prepare noodles in step 6 while reheating soup.*

corned beef
& red cabbage sandwiches

PREP TIME 20 MINUTES **COOK TIME** 6 HOURS (+ STANDING) **MAKES** 8

FIVE INGREDIENTS

¼ medium red cabbage (225g)

¼ cup (55g) brown sugar

1kg (2lb) piece corned silverside

16 slices seeded rye bread (720g)

8 slices swiss cheese (160g)

STAPLES

1 cup (250ml) red wine vinegar

1 teaspoon sea salt flakes

freshly ground black pepper

80g (2½oz) butter

1 Preheat slow cooker on HIGH.

2 Thinly slice cabbage.

3 Combine vinegar, 1½ cups (375ml) water, the sugar, salt and pepper in slow cooker. Place beef in centre of cooker, fat-side up; arrange cabbage around beef. Cook, covered, for 6 hours. Transfer beef to a large plate or tray; rest for 10 minutes. Cut into thin slices.

4 Meanwhile, just before serving, heat oven grill (broiler) on high. Spread bread slices with softened butter; grill for 1 minute on each side. Top half the bread slices with cheese; grill for 1 minute or until melted. Divide sliced corned beef among melted cheese toasts, then top with cabbage and remaining bread slices.

5 Serve sandwiches straight away.

MAKE IT SIX *Spread dijonnaise or your favourite mustard over the remaining bread slices before placing on top of the corned beef and cabbage.*

STORE IT *Refrigerate corned beef and cabbage in separate airtight containers for up to 3 days. Recipe is not suitable to freeze.*

chinese-style poached chicken

PREP TIME 25 MINUTES COOK TIME 2 HOURS 40 MINUTES (+ STANDING) SERVES 4

FIVE INGREDIENTS

1 bunch green onions (scallions)

120g (4oz) piece fresh ginger

5 cloves garlic

1.6kg (3¼lb) whole chicken

¼ cup (60ml) chinese cooking wine (shao hsing)

STAPLES

sea salt flakes

freshly ground black pepper

¼ cup (60ml) vegetable oil

1 Preheat a 5-litre (20-cup) slow cooker on HIGH.

2 Separate white and green parts of green onions; reserve 3 tops. Peel ginger; coarsely chop 100g (3oz). Crush garlic.

3 Pat chicken dry with paper towel; season cavity well. Pound the white part of the onion, chopped ginger and garlic with a large mortar and pestle (alternatively, turn a cook's knife on its side and pound each ingredient on a chopping board). Fill chicken cavity with ginger mixture, then add wine. Tie chicken legs together with kitchen string. Place in slow cooker, breast-side up; cover with 3 litres (12 cups) water. Season generously; cover with a large piece of baking paper. Cook, covered, for 2 hours 30 minutes.

4 Transfer chicken carefully to a plate; cover loosely with foil to keep warm. Stand for 10 minutes.

5 Meanwhile, finely grate remaining ginger into a small heatproof bowl; add finely chopped reserved green onion tops. Heat oil in a small saucepan over medium-high heat until just smoking; pour carefully over ginger mixture. Season well with salt.

6 Remove skin from chicken, if preferred. Cut chicken into eight pieces using a sharp cook's knife, cleaver or kitchen scissors.

7 Top chicken with ginger mixture and season with pepper; serve.

MAKE IT SIX *Use the poaching liquid to cook rice, following packet directions, if you like.*

SERVE IT *with the steamed ginger rice on page 192 and steamed asian greens on page 26, if you like.*

STORE IT *Refrigerate chicken and sauce in separate airtight containers for up to 2 days. Refrigerate the strained cooking liquid for up to 3 days, or freeze for up to 3 months; use as a stock to make soups or stews.*

one-pot spaghetti & meatballs

PREP TIME 10 MINUTES **COOK TIME** 4 HOURS **SERVES** 4

FIVE INGREDIENTS

1 medium onion (150g)

500g (1lb) flavoured thick beef sausages

800g (1½lb) bottled tomato passata

5 sprigs lemon thyme

300g (9½oz) spaghetti

STAPLES

1 tablespoon olive oil

sea salt flakes

freshly ground black pepper

1 Thinly slice onion. Remove casings from sausages; break each sausage into three pieces.

2 Heat oil in a 5-litre (20-cup) slow cooker on 'sear' (HIGH) setting. Cook meatballs, turning, for 5 minutes or until browned. Transfer to a bowl. Cook onion for 5 minutes or until golden. Return meatballs to slow cooker; add passata, thyme and 2¾ cups (680ml) water. Adjust setting to HIGH; cook, covered, for 3 hours 30 minutes.

3 Remove lid; add spaghetti to slow cooker (break in half to fit, if necessary). Stir to cover with sauce. Cook, covered, for a further 20 minutes or until spaghetti is tender; add a little boiling water to thin sauce, if necessary. Season to taste.

4 Top with extra lemon thyme to serve, if you like.

MAKE IT SIX *Top with grated parmesan to serve.*

SERVE IT *with the simple green salad on page 106 and the broccoli pesto on page 168 spooned on top, if you like.*

pork ribs with apricot & brandy

PREP TIME 15 MINUTES **COOK TIME** 5 HOURS 10 MINUTES **SERVES** 4

FIVE INGREDIENTS

2kg (4lb) American-style pork ribs

10 shallots

4cm (1½in) piece fresh ginger

275g (9oz) jar peach, mango & apricot chutney

¼ cup (60ml) brandy

STAPLES

2 tablespoons white wine vinegar

sea salt flakes

freshly ground black pepper

1 Preheat slow cooker on HIGH.

2 Cut ribs into sections, if you like. Peel 8 shallots, keeping them whole. Peel ginger; cut into fine matchsticks.

3 Place ribs, peeled shallots, ginger, chutney, brandy, 1 tablespoon of the vinegar and ½ cup (125ml) water in slow cooker. Season; mix well to coat pork evenly. Press down on ribs as much as possible to ensure they are submerged in chutney mixture. Cover with a piece of baking paper. Cook, covered, for 5 hours or until pork meat is tender. Skim and discard fat. Transfer cooking liquid to a large frying pan; boil for 10 minutes or until reduced by half.

4 Meanwhile, to make shallot pickle, thinly slice remaining shallots into rings using a mandoline or V-slicer. Place shallot in a small bowl with remaining vinegar and 1 teaspoon salt; gently massage to soften. Stand for 10 minutes for shallot to pickle.

5 Serve ribs and sauce with shallot pickle; season with pepper.

SERVE IT *with the classic coleslaw on page 106 or corn cobs with parmesan and paprika on page 26, if you like.*

STORE IT *Refrigerate rib mixture and shallot pickle in separate airtight containers for up to 3 days. Recipe is not suitable to freeze.*

4 easy *vegie sides*

1

SHAKE & BAKE WEDGES

prep + cook time 50 minutes **serves** 4

Preheat oven to 220°C/425°F. Line a large oven tray with baking paper; brush paper with 1 tablespoon olive oil. Cut 2 small orange sweet potatoes, 2 large parsnips and 2 large potatoes into wedges; toss with 1 teaspoon each smoked paprika and sea salt flakes. Spread wedges over tray. Bake for 40 minutes or until tender.

2

MINTED GREENS

prep + cook time 10 minutes **serves** 4

Cook 200g (6½oz) trimmed baby green beans and 200g (6½oz) sugar snap peas in a saucepan of boiling water for 3 minutes; drain, then transfer to a bowl. Combine ½ cup finely chopped fresh mint and 2 tablespoons extra virgin olive oil in a small bowl. Toss vegetables with mint mixture; season to taste.

3

STEAMED ASIAN GREENS

prep + cook time 15 minutes **serves** 4

Layer 350g (11oz) trimmed broccolini, 2 halved baby buk choy and 1 thinly sliced fresh long red chilli in a large baking-paper-lined bamboo steamer. Steam, covered, over a wok of simmering water for 5 minutes or until vegetables are just tender. Combine 2 tablespoons oyster sauce and 2 tablespoons boiling water in a bowl; drizzle over vegetables. Scatter with 1 teaspoon toasted sesame seeds.

4

CORN COBS WITH PARMESAN & PAPRIKA

prep + cook time 20 minutes **serves** 4

Remove silks and trim husks of 4 corn cobs. Cook corn on a heated oiled grill plate (or barbecue or grill) over medium heat, turning occasionally, for 10 minutes or until grill marks appear. Drizzle corn with 1 tablespoon extra virgin olive oil; scatter with ½ cup grated parmesan and sprinkle with 1 teaspoon smoked paprika. Season to taste. Serve with lime wedges.

vegiesides

beef & pumpkin tagine

PREP TIME 20 MINUTES **COOK TIME** 3 HOURS 10 MINUTES **SERVES** 4

FIVE INGREDIENTS

800g (1½lb) diced beef chuck steak

1kg (2lb) kent pumpkin

2 fresh long green chillies

1 tablespoon garam masala

250g (8oz) packet pearl couscous

STAPLES

2 tablespoons extra virgin olive oil

sea salt flakes

freshly ground black pepper

1 Preheat slow cooker on HIGH.

2 Trim beef of excess fat; cut into 4cm (1½in) pieces. Cut unpeeled pumpkin into 4cm (1½in) thick wedges. Thinly slice chillies; reserve one for serving (remove the seeds, if you prefer).

3 Place remaining sliced chilli, the beef, pumpkin, garam masala and oil in slow cooker. Season; turn to ensure beef and pumpkin are well coated. Add ½ cup (125ml) water to cooker. Cook, covered, for 3 hours. Season to taste.

4 Transfer pumpkin and beef to a large plate or tray using a slotted spoon. Reserve ¼ cup of the liquid. Measure remaining liquid left in the slow cooker and add enough boiling water to make 2 cups. Add in couscous in a steady stream, season, then quickly close lid. Cook, covered, for a further 10 minutes or until couscous is cooked.

5 Divide couscous among bowls; top with beef, pumpkin and reserved chilli; drizzle with reserved cooking liquid. Season; serve.

MAKE IT SIX *Add 1 finely chopped onion at the start of step 3.*

SERVE IT *topped with the lime yoghurt on page 168, if you like.*

STORE IT *Refrigerate beef and pumpkin mixture for up to 2 days. Recipe is not suitable to freeze.*

mexican chicken stew

PREP TIME 10 MINUTES **COOK TIME** 3 HOURS 45 MINUTES **SERVES** 4

FIVE INGREDIENTS

4 chicken marylands (1.4kg) or 8 thigh cutlets (1.6kg)

2 x 300g (9½oz) jars mexican chunky salsa

400g (12½oz) can four-bean mix

2 medium avocados (500g)

8 mini flour tortillas (160g)

STAPLES

1 tablespoon olive oil

sea salt flakes

freshly ground black pepper

1 Heat oil in a 5-litre (20-cup) slow cooker on 'sear' (HIGH) setting. Cook chicken for 5 minutes or until golden.

2 Add salsa to slow cooker. Adjust setting to HIGH; cook, covered, for 3 hours 30 minutes or until sauce is thickened and chicken is very tender. Remove chicken from cooker. Drain, then rinse beans; stir into sauce. Cook, covered, until heated through. Season to taste. When chicken is cool enough to handle, shred meat.

3 Chop avocados. Serve chicken with chargrilled or warmed tortillas and avocado; season with pepper.

SERVE IT *with the simple green salad or classic coleslaw on page 106 and the spiced lime yoghurt or chunky guacamole on page 168, if you like.*

STORE IT *Refrigerate stew in an airtight container for up to 2 days, or freeze for up to 3 months; thaw in the fridge.*

pork & dill cabbage rolls

PREP TIME 20 MINUTES **COOK TIME** 2 HOURS 30 MINUTES **MAKES** 16

FIVE INGREDIENTS

1kg (2lb) flavoured pork sausages

1½ cups (300g) white long-grain rice

¾ cup chopped fresh dill

1 large wombok (napa cabbage) (1.3kg)

1kg (2lb) arrabbiata pasta sauce

STAPLES

2 tablespoons extra virgin olive oil

2 tablespoons red wine vinegar

sea salt flakes

freshly ground black pepper

1 Preheat a rectangular slow cooker on HIGH (see tip).

2 Meanwhile, remove sausage meat from casings into a large bowl. Add rinsed and drained rice, ½ cup of the dill, the oil and vinegar; season. Mix well to break up sausage meat; divide into 16 portions.

3 Trim white stalks from 16 wombok leaves. Place leaves on a clean work surface. Place one portion of pork mixture on each cabbage leaf; roll once, fold in sides, then roll up firmly to enclose filling.

4 Mix pasta sauce with 1½ cups (375ml) water; spread half over base of slow cooker. Place cabbage rolls on sauce in two rows. Top with remaining sauce mixture. Cook, covered, for 2 hours 30 minutes or until cabbage rolls are cooked through.

5 Top cabbage rolls with remaining dill; season and serve.

tip You can use another shape of slow cooker, if you like, but you may need to stack the rolls and the result will be slightly different.

MAKE IT SIX *Mix sour cream with a little extra chopped dill and serve it with the rolls.*

STORE IT *Refrigerate in an airtight container for up to 3 days, or freeze for up to 3 months; thaw in the fridge.*

buffalo chicken wings

PREP TIME 15 MINUTES **COOK TIME** 1 HOUR 45 MINUTES **SERVES** 4

FIVE INGREDIENTS

2kg (4lb) chicken wing nibbles (see tip)

⅓ cup (80ml) extra hot chilli sauce

½ cup (140g) barbecue sauce

4 lebanese cucumbers (520g)

1 cup (280g) Greek-style yoghurt

STAPLES

1 tablespoon extra virgin olive oil

1 tablespoon balsamic vinegar

sea salt flakes

freshly ground black pepper

1 Preheat a 7-litre (28-cup) slow cooker on HIGH.

2 Place wings, chilli sauce, ⅓ cup of the barbecue sauce, the oil and vinegar in slow cooker; mix well. Ensure wings are in an even layer. Cook, covered, for 1 hour 30 minutes. Carefully transfer wings to a large oven tray.

3 Preheat oven grill (broiler); grill wings until golden all over.

4 Meanwhile, remove flameproof insert of slow cooker (or transfer sauce to a saucepan) and place on the stovetop, or adjust slow cooker to 'reduce' (HIGH) setting. Simmer sauce, uncovered, for 7 minutes or until reduced slightly and thickened. Pour over grilled wings.

5 Cut cucumbers into quarters lengthways. Swirl remaining barbecue sauce through yoghurt.

6 Season wings; serve with yoghurt sauce and cucumber.

tip Chicken wing nibbles are prepared chicken wings separated at the joints, with the wingtips discarded. Use the same weight of whole chicken wings, if preferred.

PREP IT *Combine wings with sauces, oil and vinegar following instructions in step 2 the day before and refrigerate, covered. Transfer wings and marinade to a preheated slow cooker and continue with the recipe.*

SERVE IT *with the perfect potato salad, classic coleslaw or lemony lettuce wedges on page 106, if you like.*

braised beef
with bacon, tomato & onion

PREP TIME 15 MINUTES **COOK TIME** 4 HOURS 50 MINUTES **SERVES** 4

FIVE INGREDIENTS

4 stems fresh flat-leaf parsley

1.3kg (2¾lb) piece beef bolar blade roast

500g (1lb) streaky bacon

240g (7½oz) jar caramelised onions

260g (8½oz) sweet berry truss tomatoes (see tip)

STAPLES

2 tablespoons red wine vinegar

sea salt flakes

freshly ground black pepper

1 Preheat a 5-litre (20-cup) slow cooker on 'sear' (HIGH) setting.

2 Separate parsley stalks and leaves. Finely chop parsley stalks to yield ¼ cup; reserve leaves for serving.

3 Trim beef of excess fat. Reserve 8 rashers bacon; cut remainder into 3cm (1¼in) pieces. Transfer bacon pieces and chopped parsley to slow cooker; cook, uncovered, stirring, for 10 minutes or until golden.

4 Add beef, caramelised onion and vinegar to slow cooker; season with salt and pepper. Stir to mix well. Add ¾ cup (180ml) boiling water. Place reserved bacon slices across top of beef, slightly overlapping each one to cover beef completely.

5 Adjust setting to HIGH; cook, covered, for 4 hours. Add tomatoes with vine intact to slow cooker; cook, covered, for further 30 minutes or until beef is very tender. Transfer beef and tomatoes to a plate; cover loosely with foil to keep warm. Transfer cooking liquid to a large frying pan; simmer, uncovered, for 10 minutes or until reduced by half. Season to taste.

6 Transfer beef to a platter; top with reserved parsley leaves and season with pepper. Serve with tomatoes and onion sauce.

tip If you can't find sweet berry truss tomatoes, use regular cherry truss tomatoes instead.

SERVE IT *with one of the mashes on page 66 and lemony lettuce wedges on page 106, if you like.*

STORE IT *Refrigerate beef in an airtight container for up to 3 days. Recipe is not suitable to freeze.*

butter chicken

PREP TIME 15 MINUTES **COOK TIME** 3 HOURS 30 MINUTES **SERVES** 4

FIVE INGREDIENTS

8 skinless chicken thigh cutlets (1.6kg) (see tip)

2 x 450g (14½oz) jars butter chicken simmer sauce

400g (12½oz) can diced tomatoes

¼ cup mint leaves

1 cup (280g) tzatziki

STAPLES

sea salt flakes

freshly ground black pepper

1 Trim and discard excess fat from chicken.

2 Heat slow cooker on HIGH. Add chicken, simmer sauce and canned tomatoes. Cook, covered, for 3 hours 30 minutes or until sauce reduces and chicken is very tender. Skim any fat from the surface with a spoon; discard. Season to taste.

3 Top butter chicken with mint and season with pepper; serve with tzatziki.

tip If the chicken cutlets come with skin, remove the skin. Place skin flat on a tray; refrigerate, uncovered, overnight. Bake in 220°C/425°F oven for 15 minutes or until golden and crisp. Serve with butter chicken.

MAKE IT SIX *Add 2 cinnamon sticks or 1 coarsely chopped onion in step 2, if you like.*

SERVE IT *with the almond pilaf on page 192 or garlic naan on page 130, if you like.*

STORE IT *Refrigerate chicken in an airtight container for up to 2 days, or freeze for 2 months; thaw in the fridge.*

almond & saffron chicken broth

PREP TIME 15 MINUTES **COOK TIME** 3 HOURS 10 MINUTES **SERVES** 4

FIVE INGREDIENTS

8 chicken thigh fillets (1.4kg)

1 teaspoon saffron threads

2 medium red onions (340g)

2 medium fennel bulbs (600g)

⅓ cup (25g) roasted flaked almonds

STAPLES

20g (¾oz) butter

sea salt flakes

freshly ground black pepper

1 tablespoon white wine vinegar

1 Preheat slow cooker on HIGH.

2 Pat chicken dry with paper towel.

3 Place 2½ cups (625ml) boiling water in a heatproof jug; add saffron threads and stir gently.

4 Peel onions; cut crossways into 1cm (½in) thick slices. Remove stalks and fronds from fennel bulbs; reserve. Cut fennel bulb crossways into 1cm (½in) thick rounds.

5 Melt butter in slow cooker. Layer onion and fennel in cooker; top with chicken. Pour over saffron mixture; season. Cook, covered, for 3 hours or until chicken and vegetables are tender. If chicken is not covered in liquid, turn over halfway through cooking.

6 Stir in vinegar; season to taste. Tear chicken into pieces. Scatter with almonds and reserved fennel fronds. Season with pepper; serve.

MAKE IT SIX *Add scrubbed halved kipfler (fingerling) potatoes with other vegetables in step 5.*

SERVE IT *with the grilled sourdough or cheddar toast on page 130. Top with almond gremolata on page 168, if you like.*

chilli con carne & cornbread 'pie'

PREP TIME 15 MINUTES **COOK TIME** 4 HOURS 10 MINUTES **SERVES** 4

FIVE INGREDIENTS

800g (1½lb) beef flank steak

3 x 425g (13½oz) cans mexe beans

2 cups (300g) self-raising flour

400g (12½oz) can creamed corn

1 cup (120g) grated smoked cheddar

STAPLES

1 tablespoon extra virgin olive oil

sea salt flakes

freshly ground black pepper

50g (1½oz) butter

1 Preheat slow cooker on HIGH.

2 Trim and discard excess fat from beef; cut into 2cm (¾in) pieces. Add oil, beef and beans (including the sauce) to slow cooker; season. Cook, covered, for 4 hours. Season to taste.

3 After bean mixture has cooked for 3 hours, place flour, diced butter and 1 teaspoon salt in a bowl. Rub flour and butter together your using fingertips until mixture reaches a sand consistency. Add creamed corn and half the cheddar; mix to form a soft dough. Divide dough into 12 pieces; roll into balls. Place balls on top of bean mixture; scatter with remaining cheese. Cook, covered, for a further 1 hour until cornbread is cooked through. Season with pepper; serve.

MAKE IT SIX *Add the chopped white part of 4 green onions (scallions) with the meat and beans in step 2, then mix the chopped green tops through the cornbread mixture.*

SERVE IT *with the simple green salad on page 106 or chunky guacamole on page 168, if you like.*

deep-pan pepperoni pizza

PREP TIME 10 MINUTES **COOK TIME** 5 HOURS **SERVES** 4

FIVE INGREDIENTS

500g (1lb) pizza dough (see tip)

80g (2½oz) sliced pepperoni

½ cup (130g) thick pasta sauce (see tip)

⅔ cup (65g) grated pizza cheese

½ cup fresh basil leaves

STAPLES

olive-oil spray

1 Preheat slow cooker on LOW.

2 Remove slow cooker insert from base and line with foil; spray foil well with oil. Remove dough from packets and knead together lightly to form a ball. Place dough in insert. Return insert to slow cooker. Cook, covered, for 45 minutes to prove.

3 Adjust setting to HIGH. Push dough down lightly, pressing it out towards the side of insert to cover the base and create a thick rim. Place half the pepperoni over base. Spread over pasta sauce, then top with remaining pepperoni and the cheese. Cook, covered, for 4 hours.

4 Preheat oven grill (broiler) on medium.

5 Remove pizza from slow cooker; place on an oven tray. Grill for 10 minutes or until cheese and crust are browned.

6 Top pizza with basil; serve straight away.

tip We used ready-made pizza dough and a fresh pasta sauce from the refrigerator section of supermarkets.

SWAP IT *Use sliced salami or ham instead of pepperoni, if you like.*

SERVE IT *with the simple green salad on page 106, if you like.*

chicken & sticky rice hotpot

PREP TIME 15 MINUTES **COOK TIME** 3 HOURS 30 MINUTES (+ REFRIGERATION) **SERVES** 4

FIVE INGREDIENTS

3 x 4cm (1½in) pieces fresh ginger

½ cup (175g) kecap manis

1.5kg (3lb) chicken wing nibbles (see tip)

1¼ cups (250g) brown rice

2 bunches baby pak choy (280g)

STAPLES

¼ cup (60ml) rice wine vinegar

2 teaspoons extra virgin olive oil

1 Grate 1 piece of ginger into a large bowl. Add ¼ cup of the kecap manis, 2 tablespoons of the vinegar and the chicken; toss well to combine. Cover; refrigerate for 4 hours or overnight.

2 Preheat slow cooker on HIGH. Add oil to cooker. When oil is hot, cook chicken in two batches, turning, for 10 minutes or until browned all over. Remove from cooker; discard marinade.

3 Finely grate another piece of ginger. Combine grated ginger, rice, 2½ cups (625ml) water, remaining kecap manis and remaining vinegar in slow cooker, spreading rice evenly over base of cooker.

4 Cook, covered, for 1 hour 30 minutes. Top rice with chicken wings; cook, covered, for a further 1 hour 30 minutes or until rice is sticky around the edges and tender in the centre and chicken is cooked.

5 Cut remaining piece of ginger into julienne. Cut each pak choy in half lengthways; wash well. Place, cut-side down, on chicken and scatter over julienned ginger. Cover; cook for a further 10 minutes or until greens are just wilted. Serve.

tip Chicken wing nibbles are prepared chicken wings separated at the joints, with the wingtips discarded. Use the same weight of whole chicken wings, if preferred.

MAKE IT SIX *Drizzle with sriracha sauce to serve.*

PREP IT *Marinate the chicken the day before; keep, covered, in the fridge.*

SERVE IT *with the steamed asian greens on page 26, if you like.*

ginger-beer-glazed ham

PREP TIME 15 MINUTES **COOK TIME** 2 HOURS 40 MINUTES **SERVES** 6

FIVE INGREDIENTS

2.5kg (5¼lb) ham (see tip)

2 cups (500ml) ginger beer

4 star anise

½ cup (170g) ginger marmalade

12 slices sourdough bread (600g)

STAPLES

¼ cup (60ml) apple cider vinegar

¼ cup (60ml) extra virgin olive oil

1 Preheat slow cooker on HIGH (see tip).

2 Remove and discard rind from ham. Using a sharp knife, score 1cm (½in) lines diagonally across ham.

3 To make glaze, place ginger beer, star anise and marmalade in slow cooker; stir to combine. Bring to the boil; simmer for 5 minutes.

4 Adjust slow cooker to LOW. Place a wire rack into cooker; place ham on wire rack. Cook, covered, for 2 hours, basting occasionally with glaze. Transfer ham to a baking-paper-lined oven tray; cover loosely with foil to keep warm.

5 Preheat oven to 200°C/400°F.

6 Add vinegar to glaze in slow cooker. Adjust setting to 'reduce' (HIGH); boil, uncovered, for 15 minutes or until reduced and thickened. Skim off fat. Brush glaze over ham. Bake ham in oven for 15 minutes or until lightly golden.

7 Meanwhile, lightly brush bread with oil. Heat a grill pan over high heat. Toast bread until grill marks appear.

8 Serve ham on toast and drizzle with remaining glaze.

tip Before you buy the ham, make sure it will fit inside your slow cooker.

SERVE IT *with the classic coleslaw or perfect potato salad on page 106, if you like.*

STORE IT *Refrigerate ham, covered, for up to 5 days, or cut into slices and freeze in an airtight container for up to 1 month.*

braised chicken
with mustard & leeks

PREP TIME 15 MINUTES **COOK TIME** 3 HOURS 50 MINUTES **SERVES** 4

FIVE INGREDIENTS

1.3kg (2¾lb) whole chicken

2 large leeks (1kg)

4 sprigs fresh tarragon

⅓ cup (95g) wholegrain mustard

250g (8oz) sour cream

STAPLES

sea salt flakes

freshly ground black pepper

1 tablespoon olive oil

1 Preheat slow cooker on 'sear' (HIGH) setting.

2 Pat chicken dry with paper towel. Place chicken, breast-side down, on a chopping board; cut down either side of the backbone using kitchen scissors. Discard backbone. Turn chicken over; cut down centre of the breast bone to split the chicken into two pieces. Press onto leg joint to break; cut around through the joint with scissors on each thigh bone to give two marylands and two breast pieces. Season chicken well.

3 Heat oil in slow cooker; add chicken, skin-side down. Cook, uncovered, turning, for 5 minutes or until golden.

4 Meanwhile trim leeks; wash thoroughly. Cut each leek on the diagonal into four large pieces. Pick tarragon leaves from stalks to yield ⅓ cup.

5 Add leek, tarragon and mustard to slow cooker; stir gently to combine. Adjust setting to HIGH; cook, covered, for 3 hours 45 minutes or until chicken is cooked through and tender.

6 Transfer chicken pieces and leek to a platter. Add sour cream to slow cooker; whisk to make a smooth sauce. Season to taste. Spoon sauce over chicken and leek. Top with extra tarragon and season with pepper, if you like; serve.

SWAP IT *Use 4 chicken marylands instead of cutting up a whole chicken, if preferred.*

SERVE IT *with one of the mashes on page 66, if you like.*

STORE IT *Refrigerate in an airtight container for up to 2 days. Recipe is suitable to freeze at the end of step 5 for 3 months; thaw in the fridge, reheat, then add the sour cream.*

asian pulled pork sliders

PREP TIME 15 MINUTES **COOK TIME** 4 HOURS 30 MINUTES **SERVES** 6

FIVE INGREDIENTS

2kg (4lb) pork rashers

10cm (4in) piece fresh ginger

¾ cup (180ml) soy sauce

⅓ cup (75g) firmly packed brown sugar

12 bake-at-home white dinner rolls (440g)

STAPLES

1 tablespoon olive oil

¾ cup (180ml) rice wine vinegar

1 Preheat slow cooker on HIGH.

2 Trim and discard excess fat from pork. Peel ginger; cut into fine matchsticks.

3 Heat oil in slow cooker; cook pork, turning, for 5 minutes or until browned all over.

4 Combine vinegar, soy sauce, sugar and ginger in a jug; pour over pork. Turn pork to coat with sauce. Cook, covered, for 4 hours or until pork is very tender. Transfer pork to a large bowl; cover loosely with foil to keep warm.

5 Adjust setting to 'reduce' (HIGH); bring sauce to the boil; cook for 25 minutes or until sauce reduces and thickens. Skim off fat. Meanwhile, shred pork. Pour sauce over pork; stir to combine.

6 To serve, split rolls in half and fill with pork; drizzle with sauce.

MAKE IT SIX *Add a packet of coleslaw mix, dressed with extra olive oil and rice wine vinegar, to the sliders, if you like.*

SERVE IT *with the classic coleslaw on page 106 and with a drizzle of sriracha sauce, if you like.*

hearty ham hock
& bean soup

PREP TIME 10 MINUTES **COOK TIME** 5 HOURS 40 MINUTES **SERVES** 4

FIVE INGREDIENTS

2 medium onions (300g)

3 large carrots (540g)

750g (1½lb) ham hock

2 litres (8 cups) chicken stock

1 cup (220g) lentils, freekeh & beans superblend

STAPLES

2 tablespoons extra virgin olive oil

sea salt flakes

freshly ground black pepper

1 Preheat slow cooker on 'sear' (HIGH) setting.

2 Finely chop onions. Dice carrots.

3 Add oil to slow cooker; cook onion, uncovered, for 5 minutes or until softened. Add ham hock and stock; cook, covered, for 4 hours 30 minutes.

4 Add superblend and carrot; cook, covered, for a further 1 hour or until tender.

5 Transfer hock to a plate; cool slightly. Remove ham meat from hock and shred. Return ham to soup. Season to taste; serve.

MAKE IT SIX *Add 2 finely chopped celery stalks with the carrot in step 4, if you like.*

SERVE IT *with the cheddar toast or grilled sourdough on page 130, if you like.*

lamb with quince & rosemary

PREP TIME 20 MINUTES **COOK TIME** 3 HOURS 15 MINUTES **SERVES** 4

FIVE INGREDIENTS

2 bunches mixed dutch (baby) carrots (800g)

1kg (2lb) lamb rump steaks

200g (6½oz) quince paste

10 x 10cm (4in) stalks fresh rosemary

4 cloves garlic

STAPLES

2 tablespoons extra virgin olive oil

1½ tablespoons balsamic vinegar

sea salt flakes

freshly ground black pepper

1 Preheat a 5-litre (20-cup) slow cooker on 'sear' (HIGH) setting.

2 Peel and trim carrots, leaving 1cm (½in) of green tops intact. Reserve ½ cup carrot tops; wash and pat dry.

3 Trim half the fat from steaks; discard. Place steaks and quince paste in a large bowl; mix to coat lamb.

4 Remove rosemary leaves from stalks; finely chop leaves to yield 2 tablespoons. Crush garlic; add half the rosemary and the garlic to lamb mixture. Mix well to coat.

5 Add lamb steaks, in batches, to slow cooker, fat-edge down; cook for 5 minutes or until dark golden. Return all lamb to cooker.

6 Adjust setting to HIGH. Add ½ cup (125ml) water, carrots, 1 tablespoon of the vinegar and any remaining quince mixture to slow cooker; stir to mix well. Season well with salt and pepper. Cook, covered, for 3 hours or until carrots and lamb are tender.

7 Meanwhile, to make carrot-top salsa, process reserved carrot tops until finely chopped; combine with remaining chopped rosemary, remaining vinegar and oil. Season to taste.

8 Adjust setting to 'reduce' (HIGH). Remove lid; bring to a simmer. Simmer for 5 minutes or until sauce thickens and coats lamb. Spoon over carrot-top salsa and scatter with extra carrot tops, if you like; serve.

SERVE IT *with the basic mashed potato or cheesy polenta on page 66, if you like.*

STORE IT *Refrigerate in an airtight container for up to 3 days. Recipe is suitable to freeze at the end of step 6 for up to 3 months; thaw in the fridge.*

chicken & biscuits

PREP TIME 25 MINUTES **COOK TIME** 2 HOURS 40 MINUTES **SERVES** 6

FIVE INGREDIENTS

1kg (2lb) chicken thigh fillets

2 medium leeks (700g)

2 bunches fresh flat-leaf parsley

500g (1lb) packaged scone mix

300g (9½oz) frozen mixed vegetables

STAPLES

50g (1½oz) butter

sea salt flakes

freshly ground black pepper

1 Trim and discard excess fat from chicken; cut into 2cm (¾in) pieces. Wash white part of leeks well; slice thinly. Wash parsley; separate leaves and stalks. Reserve small parsley leaves for serving; chop enough leaves to yield ¼ cup. Finely chop stalks.

2 Melt butter in a 5-litre (20-cup) slow cooker on 'sear' (HIGH) setting. Cook chicken, stirring, for 5 minutes or until it changes colour. Add leek and chopped parsley stalks; cook, stirring, for 3 minutes or until softened.

3 Add ¼ cup scone mix to slow cooker; cook, stirring, for 30 seconds. Gradually add 1 cup (250ml) water, stirring until combined. Season with salt and pepper; cook, covered, for 2 hours.

4 Meanwhile, place remaining scone mix in a medium bowl with chopped parsley leaves. Using a flat-bladed knife, mix in ⅔ cup (160ml) water until just combined. Turn out onto a lightly floured surface; bring dough together to form a ball. Press dough between two sheets of baking paper into a rectangle about 1.5cm (¾in) high. Remove top layer of baking paper; cut dough into 6.5cm (2¾in) squares.

5 Stir frozen vegetables into slow cooker. Place dough pieces on top of chicken mixture. Place a clean tea towel on top of cooker; replace lid. Cook, covered, for 20 minutes or until dough is cooked through.

6 Top chicken, biscuits and vegetables with reserved parsley leaves and season with pepper; serve.

MAKE IT SIX *Use chicken stock instead of water in step 3, if you like.*

SERVE IT *with the minted greens on page 26, if you like.*

harissa pork & beans

PREP TIME 15 MINUTES **COOK TIME** 5 HOURS 40 MINUTES **SERVES** 6

FIVE INGREDIENTS

1.2kg (2½lb) piece boneless pork shoulder

2 x 400g (12½oz) cans cannellini beans

½ bunch rainbow chard (375g)

6 green onions (scallions)

¼ cup (75g) harissa paste

STAPLES

2 teaspoons sea salt flakes

freshly ground black pepper

1 Preheat slow cooker on HIGH.

2 Trim and discard excess fat and skin from pork; cut into 5cm (2in) pieces.

3 Drain, then rinse beans.

4 Separate chard leaves and stalks. Cut half the stalks into 1cm (½in) thick slices; reserve leaves.

5 Using a vegetable peeler, peel remaining chard stalks into long thin strips. Place in a bowl of cold water; refrigerate to curl.

6 Trim green onions, discarding root and tip ends. Chop white part of onion into 1cm (½in) lengths. Cut green tops into 10cm (4in) lengths, then cut into long thin strips; place in a bowl of iced water to curl.

7 Place pork, beans, sliced stalks, harissa, 1 cup (250ml) water and white part of the green onion in slow cooker. Season with salt and pepper; stir until ingredients are well combined. Cook, covered, for 5 hours 30 minutes.

8 Add whole chard leaves. Cook, covered, for a further 10 minutes or until greens are wilted and pork is tender. Top with chard and green onion curls; season with pepper. Serve.

MAKE IT SIX *Use chicken stock instead of water in step 7.*

SWAP IT *Use kale or cavolo nero (tuscan cabbage) instead of rainbow chard.*

SERVE IT *with the lemon pistachio couscous on page 192 or grilled sourdough on page 130, if you like.*

san choy bau

PREP TIME 15 MINUTES **COOK TIME** 1 HOUR 15 MINUTES **SERVES** 4

FIVE INGREDIENTS

10 green onions (scallions)

1kg (2lb) minced (ground) pork

½ cup (125ml) kecap manis

1 medium iceberg lettuce (500g)

200g (6½oz) fresh singapore noodles

STAPLES

1 tablespoon peanut oil

1 Preheat slow cooker on HIGH.

2 Thinly slice 8 green onions. Add oil and sliced green onions to slow cooker; cook, uncovered, for 2 minutes.

3 Add mince; cook for 5 minutes, breaking up any lumps with the back of a wooden spoon. Stir in ⅓ cup of the kecap manis; cook, covered, for 1 hour.

4 Meanwhile, thinly slice remaining green onion lengthways; place in a bowl of iced water to curl.

5 Remove core and outer leaves of lettuce. Separate 8 lettuce leaves; soak in a large bowl of iced water for 15 minutes. Remove leaves from water; turn leaves upside down to drain. Trim to form neat cups, if you like.

6 Stir pork with a wooden spoon to break up any lumps. Top pork with noodles; cook, covered, for 5 minutes to warm noodles through.

7 Fill lettuce cups with warm mince mixture; drizzle with a little of the remaining kecap manis. Top with drained curled green onion; serve.

MAKE IT SIX *Add trimmed bean sprouts or julienned carrots to the lettuce cups in step 7, if you like.*

STORE IT *Refrigerate the pork and noodle mixture at the end of step 6 in an airtight container for up to 2 days; reheat before continuing with step 7. Recipe is not suitable to freeze.*

chicken with tahini & lemon

PREP TIME 10 MINUTES **COOK TIME** 4 HOURS 10 MINUTES **SERVES** 4

FIVE INGREDIENTS

2 large lemons (400g)

8 chicken thigh fillets (1.36kg)

⅓ cup (90g) tahini

2 tablespoons honey

½ cup fresh mint leaves

STAPLES

sea salt flakes

freshly ground black pepper

1 tablespoon extra virgin olive oil

1 Preheat a 5-litre (20-cup) slow cooker on LOW.

2 Remove lemon rind in long thin strips with a zesting tool (or using a sharp knife). Juice 1 lemon to yield ¼ cup juice. Cut remaining lemon into wedges for serving.

3 Pat chicken dry with paper towel. Combine tahini, half the lemon rind, the juice and honey in a small bowl; season with salt and pepper.

4 Transfer chicken and tahini mixture to slow cooker; cook, covered for 4 hours or until chicken is tender. Transfer chicken to a large bowl; cover loosely with foil to keep warm. Adjust setting to 'reduce' (HIGH); simmer sauce, uncovered, for 5 minutes or until thickened.

5 Season chicken to taste. Drizzle with oil and top with remaining rind and mint. Serve with lemon wedges.

SERVE IT *with the lemon pistachio couscous on page 192 and simple green salad on page 106, if you like.*

STORE IT *Refrigerate in an airtight container for up to 2 days. Recipe is not suitable to freeze.*

4 easy *mashes*

1

BASIC MASH

prep + cook time 30 minutes **serves** 4

Place 1kg (2lb) coarsely chopped potatoes in a medium saucepan with enough cold water to barely cover them. Boil over medium heat for 15 minutes or until potato is tender; drain. Return potato to pan; mash until smooth (or use a potato ricer or mouli). Add 40g (1½oz) butter and ¾ cup hot milk; fold into mash until smooth. Season to taste. Top with a little extra butter and season with pepper, if you like.

2

SWEET POTATO MASH

prep + cook time 30 minutes **serves** 4

Boil, steam or microwave 500g (1lb) each coarsely chopped peeled orange sweet potatoes and potatoes, together, until tender; drain. Mash vegetables. Combine ¼ cup chicken stock and 40g (1½oz) butter in a small saucepan over medium-high heat until butter is melted; stir into mash until combined. Season to taste. Top with a little extra butter and season with pepper, if you like.

3

MUSHY PEAS & MINT

prep + cook time 10 minutes **serves** 4

Boil, steam or microwave 500g (1lb) frozen baby green peas until just tender; drain. Blend or process peas, ½ cup firmly packed fresh mint leaves, ½ cup crème fraîche and 1 teaspoon lemon juice until almost smooth. Season to taste. Scatter with small mint leaves, if you like.

4

CHEESY POLENTA

prep + cook time 30 minutes **serves** 4

Bring 1 litre (4 cups) stock, water or milk (or half stock and half milk) to the boil in a large deep saucepan. Add 1 cup polenta in a thin steady stream, whisking until mixture comes to the boil. Reduce heat to low; cook, stirring, with a long-handled wooden spoon or whisk, for 25 minutes or until soft and thick. Stir in 30g (1oz) chopped butter and ½ cup grated parmesan; season to taste. Loosen the consistency with a little extra milk, if preferred. Scatter with extra parmesan and season with pepper, if you like.

mashes

cauliflower mac & cheese

PREP TIME 10 MINUTES **COOK TIME** 1 HOUR 20 MINUTES **SERVES** 6

FIVE INGREDIENTS

500g (1lb) cauliflower

400g (12½oz) macaroni

3½ cups (420g) grated tasty cheese

2 cups (500ml) milk

2 x 375ml cans evaporated milk

STAPLES

sea salt flakes

freshly ground black pepper

extra virgin olive oil

1 Preheat slow cooker on HIGH.

2 Cut cauliflower into small florets.

3 Add pasta, 3 cups of the cheese, milks and cauliflower to slow cooker; stir to combine. Season with salt and pepper. Cover with a piece of baking paper cut to fit slow cooker. Cook, covered, for 1 hour or until almost all the milk is absorbed, stirring halfway through cooking time.

4 Scatter over remaining cheese; cook, covered, for a further 20 minutes or until cheese melts and liquid is absorbed.

5 Serve straight away, as pasta will continue to soak up any moisture. Season to taste; drizzle with oil to serve.

MAKE IT SIX *Add 200g (6½oz) chopped bacon in step 3 or stir in 1 cup (120g) frozen peas in step 4, if you like.*

SERVE IT *with the simple green salad or lemony lettuce wedges on page 106, if you like.*

sicilian-braised lamb & eggplant

PREP TIME 15 MINUTES **COOK TIME** 3 HOURS 30 MINUTES **SERVES** 4

FIVE INGREDIENTS

8 lamb forequarter chops (1.6kg)

2 small eggplants (460g)

3 medium red onions (500g)

2 x 400g (12½oz) cans basil & garlic diced tomatoes

¾ cup (90g) marinated green sicilian olives

STAPLES

½ cup (125ml) red wine vinegar

1 Trim and discard excess fat from lamb. Cut eggplant into 3cm (1¼in) chunks. Cut 2 onions into 6 wedges each.

2 Heat slow cooker on HIGH. Add lamb, eggplant, onion wedges, canned tomatoes and olives to cooker; stir vegetables gently without moving the lamb too much. Stir in 1 tablespoon of the vinegar; cook, covered, for 3 hours 30 minutes or until lamb is tender and sauce is thick.

3 Meanwhile, thinly slice remaining onion. Place in a small bowl; cover with remaining vinegar. Stand for 2 hours.

4 Skim any fat from the surface of lamb mixture. Season to taste. Top with pickled onion; serve.

SERVE IT *with the cheesy polenta on page 66 or grilled sourdough on page 130, topped with the almond gremolata on page 168, if you like.*

STORE IT *Refrigerate in an airtight container for up to 2 days. Recipe is not suitable to freeze.*

sweet potato & speck risotto

PREP TIME 10 MINUTES **COOK TIME** 2 HOURS 10 MINUTES **SERVES** 4

FIVE INGREDIENTS

500g (1lb) speck

500g (1lb) orange sweet potato

2 cups (400g) medium-grain brown rice

1 litre (4 cups) chicken stock

150g (4½oz) piece parmesan

STAPLES

40g (1½oz) butter

sea salt flakes

freshly ground black pepper

1 Preheat a 5-litre (20-cup) slow cooker on 'sear' (HIGH) setting.

2 Trim and discard rind from speck; cut into 1cm (½in) pieces. Peel sweet potato; cut into 3cm (1¼in) pieces.

3 Melt half the butter in slow cooker; cook speck, in batches, uncovered, for 5 minutes or until browned.

4 Adjust setting to LOW. Add rice, stirring to coat grains in butter. Add sweet potato and stock; cook, covered, for 2 hours.

5 Meanwhile, finely grate parmesan. Stir ⅔ cup grated parmesan and remaining butter through risotto; season to taste.

6 Top risotto with remaining parmesan; serve.

MAKE IT SIX *Add 1 teaspoon chopped fresh thyme or rosemary with the sweet potato in step 4, and serve topped with extra of the herb, if you like.*

SERVE IT *with the simple green salad on page 106, if you like.*

asian-style beef cups

PREP TIME 5 MINUTES **COOK TIME** 5 HOURS 10 MINUTES **SERVES** 4

FIVE INGREDIENTS

1kg (2lb) minced (ground) beef

2 fresh long red chillies

4 green onions (scallions)

½ cup (125ml) kecap manis

2 baby cos (romaine) lettuce (260g)

STAPLES

1 tablespoon olive oil

2 teaspoons rice wine vinegar

1 Heat oil in a 5-litre (20-cup) slow cooker on 'sear' (HIGH) setting. Cook beef, stirring, for 5 minutes or until well browned. Drain excess oil from cooker.

2 Meanwhile, finely chop 1 chilli and half the green onions. Add chopped chilli and green onion, kecap manis and ⅓ cup (80ml) water to slow cooker. Adjust setting to LOW; cook, covered, for 5 hours. Stir in vinegar.

3 Cut remaining chilli and green onions into thin slices on the diagonal. Separate, wash and dry lettuce leaves.

4 Place spoonfuls of beef in lettuce cups; top with sliced onion and chilli. Serve.

MAKE IT SIX *Add a squeeze of lime juice to mince mixture at the end of step 2 with the vinegar and serve with lime wedges.*

STORE IT *Refrigerate mince mixture at the end of step 2 in an airtight container for up to 2 days. Continue with the recipe just before serving.*

chicken & corn dumpling stew

PREP TIME 30 MINUTES **COOK TIME** 3 HOURS 40 MINUTES **SERVES** 6

FIVE INGREDIENTS

1kg (2lb) chicken thigh fillets

4 medium carrots (500g)

3 trimmed stalks celery (300g)

535g (1lb) packaged scone mix

425g (13½oz) corn cobbettes

STAPLES

50g (1½oz) butter

sea salt flakes

freshly ground black pepper

1 Preheat slow cooker on HIGH.

2 Trim and discard excess fat from chicken thighs. Trim carrots and celery, reserving any small celery leaves. Halve carrots lengthways. Cut carrots and celery crossways on the diagonal into 5cm (2in) pieces.

3 Melt butter in slow cooker; stir in 2 tablespoons of the scone mix. Cook, stirring, for 2 minutes or until smooth. Add 2 cups (500ml) boiling water; mix well until smooth. Add chicken, carrot, celery and corn to cooker; stir to mix well. Season. Cook, covered, for 2 hours 30 minutes.

4 Use remainder of the scone mix to make scones following packet directions, using water instead of milk. Press dough out on a lightly floured surface until 3cm (1¼in) thick; cut into 6cm (2½in) scones. Re-roll scraps; press out and cut more scones.

5 Place scones on top of mixture in slow cooker. Cook, covered, for 1 hour or until scones are puffed and chicken is cooked through. Season to taste.

6 Top stew with reserved celery leaves; serve.

MAKE IT SIX *Add 3 fresh thyme sprigs with the vegetables in step 3.*

SERVE IT *with the minted greens on page 26, if you like.*

STORE IT *Refrigerate in an airtight container for up to 2 days. Recipe is not suitable to freeze.*

coconut & peanut beef

PREP TIME 20 MINUTES **COOK TIME** 5 HOURS **SERVES** 6

FIVE INGREDIENTS

1.4kg (2¾lb) beef chuck steak

½ bunch fresh coriander (cilantro)

⅔ cup (185g) smooth peanut butter

400ml can coconut milk

2½ tablespoons chilli paste

STAPLES

1 tablespoon red wine vinegar

1 tablespoon extra virgin olive oil

sea salt flakes

freshly ground black pepper

1 Preheat slow cooker on HIGH.

2 Trim and discard excess fat and sinew from beef; cut into 4cm (1½in) pieces.

3 Wash coriander well; pat dry. Pick coriander leaves in sprigs from stems; reserve leaves. Trim roots; finely chop roots to yield 2 tablespoons (make up quantity with chopped stems if not enough).

4 Combine coriander root, peanut butter, coconut milk, 2 tablespoons of the chilli paste, the vinegar and ½ cup (125ml) boiling water in slow cooker. Add beef; stir to mix well. Cook, covered, for 5 hours or until beef is tender and sauce is thickened. Transfer beef from cooker to a medium bowl with a slotted spoon. Blend sauce with a stick blender until smooth.

5 Meanwhile, combine remaining chilli paste and the oil in a small bowl.

6 Stir half the reserved coriander leaves through beef mixture; drizzle with chilli oil mixture. Season to taste. Top with remaining coriander leaves; serve.

MAKE IT SIX *Add torn fresh kaffir lime leaves in with the beef in step 4.*

SERVE IT *with the almond pilaf on page 192, if you like.*

STORE IT *Refrigerate in an airtight container for up to 2 days, or freeze for up to 3 months; thaw in the fridge.*

Under 8 hours

sticky fig lamb shanks
with fennel

PREP TIME 15 MINUTES **COOK TIME** 6 HOURS 40 MINUTES **SERVES** 6

FIVE INGREDIENTS

2 large fennel bulbs (1.1kg)

6 small lamb shanks (1.2kg)

235g (7½oz) jar fig, date & balsamic chutney

2 sticks cinnamon

700g (1½lb) baby kale

STAPLES

2 teaspoons extra virgin olive oil

sea salt flakes

freshly ground black pepper

2 tablespoons balsamic vinegar

1 Preheat a 5-litre (20-cup) slow cooker on 'sear' (HIGH) setting.

2 Cut fennel bulbs into quarters; reserve fronds.

3 Season lamb well with salt and pepper. Heat oil in slow cooker; cook lamb, turning, for 10 minutes or until browned all over. Transfer to a large bowl. Add fennel to cooker; cook for 3 minutes on each side or until browned. Transfer to bowl with lamb.

4 Add ½ cup (125ml) water, chutney and balsamic vinegar to slow cooker; cook, stirring, until combined. Stir in an extra 1½ cups (375ml) water and broken cinnamon sticks.

5 Place lamb and fennel, in even layers, in slow cooker. Adjust setting to LOW; cook, covered, for 6 hours or until lamb is very tender and just starting to fall off the bone. Add kale; cook for a further 10 minutes.

6 Transfer lamb and vegetables carefully to a tray; cover loosely with foil to keep warm. Pour cooking liquid into a large jug; skim off fat. Measure 3 cups liquid (see tip); return to slow cooker. Discard any remaining liquid in jug. Adjust setting to 'reduce' (HIGH); simmer sauce, uncovered, for 10 minutes or until thickened. (Sauce can also be simmered in a frying pan for 5 minutes.)

7 Return lamb shanks and vegetables to sauce. Serve topped with reserved fennel fronds.

tip If you don't have enough liquid in step 6, add water to make 3 cups.

SERVE IT *with the basic mash, sweet potato mash or cheesy polenta on page 66, if you like.*

STORE IT *Refrigerate in an airtight container for up to 2 days, or freeze without kale for up to 1 month; thaw in the fridge and add kale when reheating.*

veal rolls with prosciutto & sage

PREP TIME 20 MINUTES **COOK TIME** 6 HOURS 10 MINUTES **SERVES** 4

FIVE INGREDIENTS

8 slices prosciutto (120g)

8 veal schnitzels (800g)

⅔ cup (130g) drained chargrilled capsicum (bell pepper) strips

400g (12½oz) bottled tomato pasta sauce

16 sage leaves

STAPLES

⅓ cup (80ml) olive oil

sea salt flakes

freshly ground black pepper

1 Preheat a 5-litre (20-cup) slow cooker on 'sear' (HIGH) setting.

2 Place prosciutto slices on a chopping board; top each slice with a schnitzel. Place capsicum strips across centre of schnitzels. Roll to enclose filling; secure veal rolls with toothpicks or kitchen string.

3 Heat 1 tablespoon of the oil in slow cooker. Cook veal rolls, turning, for 10 minutes or until well browned. Add ¼ cup (60ml) water, the pasta sauce and 8 chopped sage leaves. Adjust setting to LOW; cook, covered, for 6 hours. Season to taste.

4 Heat remaining oil in a small saucepan. Fry remaining sage leaves for 10 seconds or until crisp. Remove sage from pan with slotted spoon; drain on paper towel.

5 Serve veal rolls with sauce, topped with crisp sage leaves.

SERVE IT *topped with the almond gremolata or broccoli pesto on page 168, or with the cheesy polenta on page 66, if you like.*

STORE IT *Refrigerate in an airtight container for up to 3 days, or freeze for up to 2 months; thaw in the fridge.*

spicy lamb meatball subs

PREP TIME 10 MINUTES **COOK TIME** 6 HOURS **SERVES** 6

FIVE INGREDIENTS

1 medium red capsicum (bell pepper) (200g)

500g (1lb) arrabbiata pasta sauce

1kg (2lb) merguez sausages

2 long baguettes (french sticks)

60g (2oz) rocket (arugula) leaves

STAPLES

sea salt flakes

freshly ground black pepper

40g (1½oz) butter

1 Halve capsicum, remove seeds and membrane, then chop coarsely.

2 Place capsicum and pasta sauce in a 5-litre (20-cup) slow cooker.

3 Heat slow cooker on LOW. Remove sausage meat from casings into a bowl. Roll level tablespoons into balls; add to cooker. Cook, covered, for 6 hours. Season to taste.

4 Cut baguettes into thirds; split and spread with butter. Fill rolls with meatballs and rocket. Season with pepper; serve.

SWAP IT *Use your favourite sausage instead of merguez and your favourite pasta sauce instead of arrabbiata for a less spicy version, if preferred.*

MAKE IT SIX *Add mozzarella or parmesan to baguettes in step 4.*

STORE IT *Refrigerate meatballs for up to 2 days, or freeze for up to 2 months; thaw in the fridge.*

brown rice biryani

PREP TIME 15 MINUTES **COOK TIME** 6 HOURS 45 MINUTES **SERVES** 6

FIVE INGREDIENTS

1kg (2lb) beef chuck steak

2 medium red onions (340g)

1 bunch fresh coriander (cilantro)

½ cup (150g) korma curry paste

2 cups (400g) brown rice

STAPLES

¼ cup (60ml) vegetable oil

sea salt flakes

freshly ground black pepper

⅓ cup (80ml) red wine vinegar

1 Trim beef of excess fat; cut into 3cm (1¼in) pieces. Finely chop one of the onions; slice remaining onion into thin rounds. Wash coriander well. Separate coriander roots, stems and leaves. Finely chop roots and stems; reserve leaves to serve.

2 Heat 1 tablespoon of the oil in a 5-litre (20-cup) slow cooker on 'sear' (HIGH) setting. Add half the beef; season with salt and pepper. Cook, uncovered, for 4 minutes or until browned all over. Transfer to a large bowl. Repeat with another 1 tablespoon oil and remaining beef.

3 Heat remaining oil in slow cooker; cook chopped onion and chopped coriander, stirring, for 3 minutes or until softened.

4 Add curry paste; cook, stirring, for 2 minutes. Add 2 cups (500ml) water, stirring to remove any caught pieces. Return beef to slow cooker; season. Adjust setting to LOW; cook, covered, for 4 hours 30 minutes.

5 Add rice and another 3 cups (750ml) water to slow cooker; stir to combine. Cook, covered, for a further 2 hours or until rice is tender.

6 Meanwhile, to make pickled red onion, combine vinegar and 1 teaspoon salt in a medium bowl. Add sliced onion; stand for 2 hours.

7 Top biryani with drained pickled onion and reserved coriander leaves; serve.

MAKE IT SIX *Use beef stock instead of water in steps 4 and 5. Or top biryani with chopped roasted cashews or Greek-style yoghurt mixed with extra chopped coriander.*

STORE IT *Refrigerate in an airtight container for up to 1 day. Recipe is not suitable to freeze.*

pomegranate-glazed lamb & pumpkin

PREP TIME 15 MINUTES **COOK TIME** 7 HOURS **SERVES** 4

FIVE INGREDIENTS

1.5kg (3lb) lamb shoulder with bone

½ cup (50g) pistachio dukkah

2 cups (500ml) pomegranate juice

800g (1½lb) kent pumpkin

1 medium pomegranate (320g)

STAPLES

1 tablespoon extra virgin olive oil

sea salt flakes

freshly ground plack pepper

2 teaspoons balsamic vinegar

1 Trim and discard excess fat from lamb. Rub half the dukkah over lamb; season well with salt and pepper.

2 Preheat oil in 5-litre (20-cup) slow cooker on 'sear' (HIGH) setting. Sear lamb for 5 minutes on each side or until browned all over.

3 Adjust setting to LOW. Add pomegranate juice to slow cooker; cook, covered, for 5 hours 45 minutes.

4 Cut unpeeled seeded pumpkin into 4cm (1½in) thick wedges. Add pumpkin to slow cooker; cook, covered, for a further 45 minutes or until pumpkin is tender.

5 Carefully transfer pumpkin and lamb to a tray or large plate; cover loosely with foil to keep warm. Adjust setting to 'reduce' (HIGH). Pour cooking liquid into a large jug; skim off fat. Measure 3 cups liquid (see tip); return to slow cooker. Discard any remaining liquid in jug. Add balsamic vinegar to cooker; bring to the boil. Simmer, uncovered, for 15 minutes or until thickened. (Or simmer liquid and vinegar in a saucepan on the stovetop.)

6 Meanwhile, to remove seeds from pomegranate, cut pomegranate in half crossways; hold it, cut-side down, in the palm of your hand over a bowl, then hit the outside firmly with a wooden spoon. The seeds should fall out easily; discard any white pith that falls out with them. Scrape out any remaining seeds. (Pomegranate seeds will keep, covered, in the fridge for up 4 days.)

7 Sprinkle lamb and pumpkin with remaining dukkah and top with pomegranate seeds; serve with sauce.

tip If you don't have enough liquid in step 5, add water to make 3 cups.

SERVE IT *with the simple green salad on page 106 or lemon pistachio couscous on page 192, if you like.*

STORE IT *Refrigerate in an airtight container for up to 3 days. Recipe is not suitable to freeze.*

sardinian lamb
with holiday beans

PREP TIME 15 MINUTES **COOK TIME** 6 HOURS 15 MINUTES **SERVES** 6

FIVE INGREDIENTS

6 medium potatoes (1.2kg)

300g (9½oz) green beans

1 medium bulb garlic

¾ cup fresh oregano leaves

1.2kg (2½lb) whole easy-carve lamb leg

STAPLES

⅓ cup (80ml) red wine vinegar

sea salt flakes

freshly ground black pepper

1 Preheat a 5-litre (20-cup) slow cooker on LOW.

2 Cut potatoes into 4cm (1½in) chunks. Trim beans. Halve whole garlic bulb crossways. Coarsely chop ½ cup of the oregano leaves. Add potato, three-quarters of the beans, the garlic, chopped oregano and vinegar to slow cooker; season with salt and pepper.

3 Place lamb on potato mixture; season lamb with salt and pepper. Add 1 cup (250ml) water to slow cooker. Cook, covered, for 6 hours 15 minutes or until lamb is slightly pink in the centre and potato is tender. Skim and discard excess fat.

4 Just before serving, slice remaining beans. Add beans to a pan of boiling salted water; return to the boil. Drain.

5 Top lamb mixture with blanched beans and remaining oregano; season to taste. Serve.

MAKE IT SIX *Add lemon wedges for serving.*

SERVE IT *topped with the broccoli pesto on page 168, if you like.*

STORE IT *Refrigerate lamb and vegetables in separate airtight containers for up to 2 days. Recipe is not suitable to freeze.*

barbecue pork chops

PREP TIME 15 MINUTES **COOK TIME** 6 HOURS 15 MINUTES **SERVES** 4

FIVE INGREDIENTS

4 pork forequarter chops (1kg)

1 large onion (200g)

3 fresh long red chillies

1 cup (250ml) barbecue sauce

¼ cup (70g) dijon mustard

STAPLES

2 tablespoons white wine vinegar

1 Trim rind and excess fat from chops, keeping them intact. Halve and thickly slice onion. Cut 2 chillies in half lengthways, leaving stems intact. Combine sauce, mustard and vinegar in a small bowl.

2 Heat slow cooker on LOW. Add pork, onion, halved chillies and barbecue sauce mixture; cook, covered, for 6 hours. Remove chops and skim surface of excess oil; discard. Transfer pork to a tray or large plate; cover loosely with foil to keep warm.

3 Adjust setting to 'reduce' (HIGH); boil sauce, uncovered, for 15 minutes or until reduced and thickened.

4 Cut remaining chilli into thin strips. Top pork chops and sauce with remaining chilli; serve.

SWAP IT *Use wholegrain or american mustard instead of dijon, if preferred.*

SERVE IT *with the classic coleslaw or perfect potato salad on page 106, or the shake and bake wedges or corn cobs with parmesan and paprika on page 26, if you like.*

beef braised with beetroot & mustard

PREP TIME 10 MINUTES **COOK TIME** 7 HOURS **SERVES** 4

FIVE INGREDIENTS

1kg (2lb) beef oyster blade steak

1kg (2lb) small beetroot (beets), with leaves if possible

½ cup (125ml) dijon mustard

1 tablespoon ground cumin

400g (12½oz) small orange sweet potato

STAPLES

1 tablespoon extra virgin olive oil

sea salt flakes

freshly ground black pepper

1   Preheat slow cooker on HIGH.

2   Trim and discard excess fat from beef; transfer to a large bowl.

3   Wash beetroot and leaves; reserve leaves. Peel beetroot. Add beetroot to bowl with beef.

4   Combine mustard, cumin and oil in a small bowl. Add to beef and beetroot; stir to coat. Season with salt and pepper.

5   Place beef in slow cooker; top with beetroot. Pour ¾ cup (180ml) water over beef and beetroot; cook, covered, for 6 hours.

6   Lightly scrub sweet potato; cut in half lengthways. Place, cut-side up, on top of beetroot. Season. Cook, covered, for 1 hour or until beef is very tender and a knife inserts easily into vegetables.

7   Cut beef into thick slices. Serve with beetroot, sweet potato and reserved beetroot leaves. Season to taste; drizzle with a little of the cooking juices. Serve.

SERVE IT *topped with the spiced lime yoghurt on page 168, if you like.*

STORE IT *Refrigerate beef and vegetables in separate airtight containers for up to 2 days. Recipe is not suitable to freeze.*

green olive & lemon chicken

PREP TIME 15 MINUTES **COOK TIME** 6 HOURS **SERVES** 4

FIVE INGREDIENTS

2 medium lemons (280g)

3 cloves garlic

¼ cup (30g) pitted green olives

⅓ cup fresh flat-leaf parsley leaves

1.5kg (3lb) whole chicken

STAPLES

15g (½oz) butter

1 tablespoon olive oil

sea salt flakes

freshly ground black pepper

1 Finely grate 1 lemon to yield 2 teaspoons rind; cut lemon into wedges. Crush garlic. Finely chop olives and parsley. Combine butter, oil, rind, garlic, olives and parsley in a medium bowl; season.

2 Pat chicken dry with paper towel. Make a pocket between breasts and skin with your fingers; push half the butter mixture under skin. Rub remaining butter mixture over chicken. Tuck wing tips under. Fill cavity with lemon wedges, then tie legs together with kitchen string. Trim skin around neck; secure neck flap to underside of chicken with small fine skewers.

3 Heat a 5-litre (20-cup) slow cooker on LOW. Place chicken in cooker; cook, covered, for 6 hours.

4 Cut chicken into quarters; season. Serve with extra parsley sprigs and remaining lemon cut into wedges.

MAKE IT SIX *Add 2 tablespoons fresh thyme leaves to the butter mixture in step 1.*

SERVE IT *with the shake and bake wedges on page 26 or one of the salads on page 106, if you like.*

rendang lamb shanks

PREP TIME 10 MINUTES **COOK TIME** 7 HOURS 30 MINUTES **SERVES** 4

FIVE INGREDIENTS

4 small french-trimmed lamb shanks (800g)

2 medium onions (300g)

6 kaffir lime leaves

185g (6oz) jar rendang curry paste

270g (8½oz) can coconut cream

STAPLES

1 tablespoon olive oil

sea salt flakes

freshly ground black pepper

1 Heat oil in a 5-litre (20-cup) slow cooker on 'sear' (HIGH) setting. Cook lamb, turning, for 15 minutes or until browned on all sides. Transfer to a plate.

2 Meanwhile, cut onions into six large wedges each. Tear 4 kaffir lime leaves. Add onion and torn kaffir lime leaves to cooker. Adjust setting to 'sear' (MEDIUM); cook, stirring, for 5 minutes. Add paste; cook for 1 minute. Stir in coconut cream and ½ cup (125ml) water until combined.

3 Return lamb to slow cooker. Adjust setting to LOW; cook, covered, for 7 hours. Season to taste.

4 Thinly slice remaining lime leaves. Top lamb shanks with sliced lime leaves; serve.

MAKE IT SIX *Add the finely chopped roots and stems from 1 bunch of coriander (cilantro) in step 2 and top shanks with the leaves in step 4.*

SERVE IT *with the steamed ginger rice or cauliflower 'rice' on page 192, if you like.*

plum & ginger chicken

PREP TIME 5 MINUTES **COOK TIME** 6 HOURS 45 MINUTES **SERVES** 4

FIVE INGREDIENTS

700g (1½lb) jar whole plums in natural juice

2cm (¾in) piece fresh ginger

2 tablespoons soy sauce

2 teaspoons chinese five spice

8 chicken lovely legs (1kg) (see tip)

STAPLES

1 tablespoon extra virgin olive oil

1 Drain plums over a bowl; reserve juice and halve the plums. Peel ginger; cut into thin matchsticks. Stir ginger, soy sauce and five spice into juice.

2 Heat oil in a 5-litre (20-cup) slow cooker on 'sear' (HIGH) setting. Cook chicken, turning, for 10 minutes or until browned all over; add juice mixture.

3 Adjust setting to LOW; cook, covered, for 6 hours 15 minutes. Transfer chicken to a bowl.

4 Adjust setting to 'reduce' (HIGH); bring sauce to the boil, then simmer, uncovered, for 10 minutes or until thickened slightly.

5 Return chicken to sauce; add plums. Cook, uncovered, for 10 minutes or until plums are heated through. Season to taste; serve.

tip Lovely legs are trimmed drumsticks with the skin removed.

SERVE IT *with the steamed asian greens on page 26 and steamed ginger rice or almond pilaf on page 192, if you like.*

STORE IT *Refrigerate in an airtight container for up to 2 days, or freeze for up to 3 months; thaw in the fridge.*

cottage pie

PREP TIME 5 MINUTES **COOK TIME** 6 HOURS 40 MINUTES (+ STANDING) **SERVES** 6

FIVE INGREDIENTS

1 medium red onion (170g)

1kg (2lb) minced (ground) beef

500g (1lb) jar tomato, onion & roast garlic pasta sauce

500g (1lb) frozen mixed vegetables

1kg (2lb) mashed potatoes (see tip)

STAPLES

1 tablespoon extra virgin olive oil

sea salt flakes

freshly ground black pepper

1 Heat oil in a rectangular slow cooker on HIGH.

2 Finely chop onion; cook for 5 minutes or until softened. Season with salt and pepper. Add half the beef and season; cook, uncovered, stirring, for 10 minutes or until well browned. Transfer to a bowl; repeat with remaining beef. Return all beef mince to slow cooker.

3 Adjust setting to LOW. Add pasta sauce and vegetables to slow cooker; stir to combine. Cook, covered, for 5 hours or until sauce is reduced.

4 Spoon mashed potato over beef mixture.

5 Cover slow cooker insert with a clean tea towel, then replace cooker lid; cook, covered, for a further 1 hour 15 minutes.

6 Stand for 10 minutes. Season; serve.

tip For convenience, we used ready-mashed potato from the refrigerated section of supermarkets.

SWAP IT *Use pork or a mixture of pork and veal instead of beef.*

SERVE IT *with the simple green salad on page 106 or minted greens on page 26, if you like.*

STORE IT *Refrigerate in an airtight container for up to 1 day. Recipe is not suitable to freeze.*

4 easy *side salads*

1

CLASSIC COLESLAW

prep time 10 minutes **serves** 4

Combine 2 tablespoons mayonnaise, 1 tablespoon white wine vinegar and 1 teaspoon wholegrain mustard. Place a 300g packet fine cut coleslaw, 1 coarsely grated medium carrot and 3 thinly sliced green onions (scallions) in a large bowl with dressing; toss gently to combine.

2

LEMONY LETTUCE WEDGES

prep time 5 minutes **serves** 4

Combine ½ cup each sour cream and mayonnaise, ½ teaspoon finely grated lemon rind and 3 teaspoons lemon juice in a small bowl. Season to taste. Wash and drain 2 quartered baby cos (romaine) lettuces. Place on a platter. Spoon mayonnaise mixture over lettuce. Scatter with 1 tablespoon chopped fresh chives and extra lemon zest.

3

SIMPLE GREEN SALAD

prep time 5 minutes **serves** 4

Place 100g (3oz) mixed salad leaves in a bowl. Top with 1 large coarsely chopped avocado and 4 thickly sliced baby cucumbers (qukes). Combine 1 tablespoon extra virgin olive oil with 2 teaspoons red wine vinegar and 1 teaspoon dijon mustard in a small bowl. Season to taste. Drizzle over salad; season.

4

PERFECT POTATO SALAD

prep + cook time 20 minutes **serves** 6

Cut 1.5kg (3lb) potatoes into large pieces. Boil, microwave or steam potato until tender; drain. Transfer to a large bowl; drizzle over 2 tablespoons apple cider vinegar. Toss gently to combine. Add ½ cup mayonnaise combined with 2 teaspoons horseradish cream. Stir in 2 tablespoons each coarsely chopped fresh mint and dill. Season to taste. Scatter with extra mint; serve.

side salads

sloppy joes

PREP TIME 5 MINUTES **COOK TIME** 6 HOURS 30 MINUTES **SERVES** 6

FIVE INGREDIENTS

1kg (2lb) minced (ground) pork and veal

1 tablespoon sweet paprika

410g (12½oz) can tomato puree

¼ cup (90g) golden syrup

6 hot dog rolls (450g)

STAPLES

2 tablespoons olive oil

½ cup (125ml) apple cider vinegar

sea salt flakes

freshly ground black pepper

30g (1oz) butter

1 Heat oil in a 5-litre (20-cup) slow cooker on 'sear' (HIGH) setting. Cook mince, in two batches, stirring, for 5 minutes or until browned. Add paprika; cook, stirring, for 1 minute or until fragrant.

2 Return mince to slow cooker. Add tomato puree, syrup and vinegar. Adjust setting to LOW; cook, covered, for 6 hours.

3 Adjust setting to 'reduce' (HIGH); simmer, uncovered, for 10 minutes or until sauce is thick. Season to taste.

4 Split hot dog rolls without cutting all the way through. Spread with butter. Spoon sloppy joe mixture into buttered rolls; serve.

SERVE IT *with the classic coleslaw on page 106, or corn cobs with parmesan and paprika or shake and bake wedges on page 26, if you like.*

STORE IT *Refrigerate mince mixture at the end of step 3 in an airtight container for up to 2 days, or freeze for up to 3 months; thaw in the fridge.*

veal with balsamic glaze

PREP TIME 5 MINUTES COOK TIME 6 HOURS 15 MINUTES SERVES 6

FIVE INGREDIENTS

6 pieces veal osso buco (1.2kg)

2 tablespoons plain (all-purpose) flour

2 cloves garlic

2 tablespoons fresh sage leaves

1 cup (250ml) chicken stock

STAPLES

2 tablespoons olive oil

½ cup (125ml) balsamic vinegar

sea salt flakes

freshly ground black pepper

1 Heat oil in a 5-litre (20-cup) slow cooker on 'sear' (HIGH) setting. Toss veal in flour to coat; shake off excess. Cook veal, in batches, for 5 minutes until browned on both sides.

2 Thinly slice garlic and chop sage. Add garlic and sage to slow cooker; cook, stirring, until fragrant. Add vinegar; boil, uncovered, for 2 minutes or until reduced by half. Stir in stock.

3 Adjust setting to LOW; cook, covered, for 6 hours. Season to taste.

4 Scatter with extra sage, if you like; serve.

SERVE IT *with the cheesy polenta or basic mash on page 66 and minted greens on page 26, if you like.*

STORE IT *Refrigerate in an airtight container for up to 3 days, or freeze for up to 3 months; thaw in the fridge.*

herby lamb leg with parmesan polenta

PREP TIME 15 MINUTES **COOK TIME** 7 HOURS 30 MINUTES **SERVES** 6

FIVE INGREDIENTS

200g (6½oz) piece parmesan

⅓ cup fresh oregano leaves

3 large red capsicums (bell peppers) (1kg)

2 cups (340g) polenta (cornmeal)

1.2kg (2½lb) marinated butterflied lamb leg

STAPLES

sea salt flakes

freshly ground black pepper

1 Preheat slow cooker on LOW.

2 Coarsely grate three-quarters of the parmesan; refrigerate remainder until needed.

3 Coarsely chop ¼ cup of the oregano leaves; reserve remainder to serve.

4 Quarter capsicums; remove seeds and membranes.

5 Pour 2.125 litres (8½ cups) boiling water into slow cooker; add polenta, grated parmesan and chopped oregano. Season; stir well. Top polenta mixture with capsicum, then place lamb in the centre. Cook, covered, for 7 hours 30 minutes or until the lamb is tender and polenta is soft.

6 Remove lamb and capsicum; cut lamb into thick slices. Whisk polenta to incorporate liquid on top. Serve lamb, capsicum and polenta scattered with remaining grated parmesan and oregano leaves; season to taste. Serve.

SERVE IT *topped with the broccoli pesto on page 168 and with the simple green salad on page 106, if you like.*

STORE IT *Refrigerate lamb and polenta in separate airtight containers for up to 2 days. This recipe is not suitable to freeze.*

char siu pork ribs

PREP TIME 5 MINUTES **COOK TIME** 7 HOURS 20 MINUTES **SERVES** 6

FIVE INGREDIENTS

2.5kg (5lb) American-style pork ribs

2 fresh long red chillies

½ cup (125ml) char siu sauce

2 tablespoons soy sauce

¼ cup (60ml) orange juice

STAPLES

2 tablespoons peanut oil

1 Heat oil in a 5-litre (20-cup) slow cooker on 'sear' (HIGH) setting. Cut ribs into pieces that will fit into cooker. Cook ribs, in batches, until browned all over.

2 Finely chop 1 chilli.

3 Combine chopped chilli, sauces and juice in a jug; brush over ribs. Adjust setting to LOW. Place ribs in slow cooker; pour over remaining sauce. Cook, covered, for 7 hours.

4 Remove ribs from sauce; cover to keep warm. Adjust setting to 'reduce' (HIGH); bring sauce to the boil. Boil for 5 minutes or until sauce is thickened slightly.

5 Meanwhile, seed remaining chilli and cut into long thin strips. Drizzle ribs with sauce and top with chilli; serve.

MAKE IT SIX *Add 2 teaspoons finely grated fresh ginger or 2 cloves crushed garlic in step 3.*

SERVE IT *with the steamed asian greens and steamed ginger rice or the shake and bake wedges on page 26.*

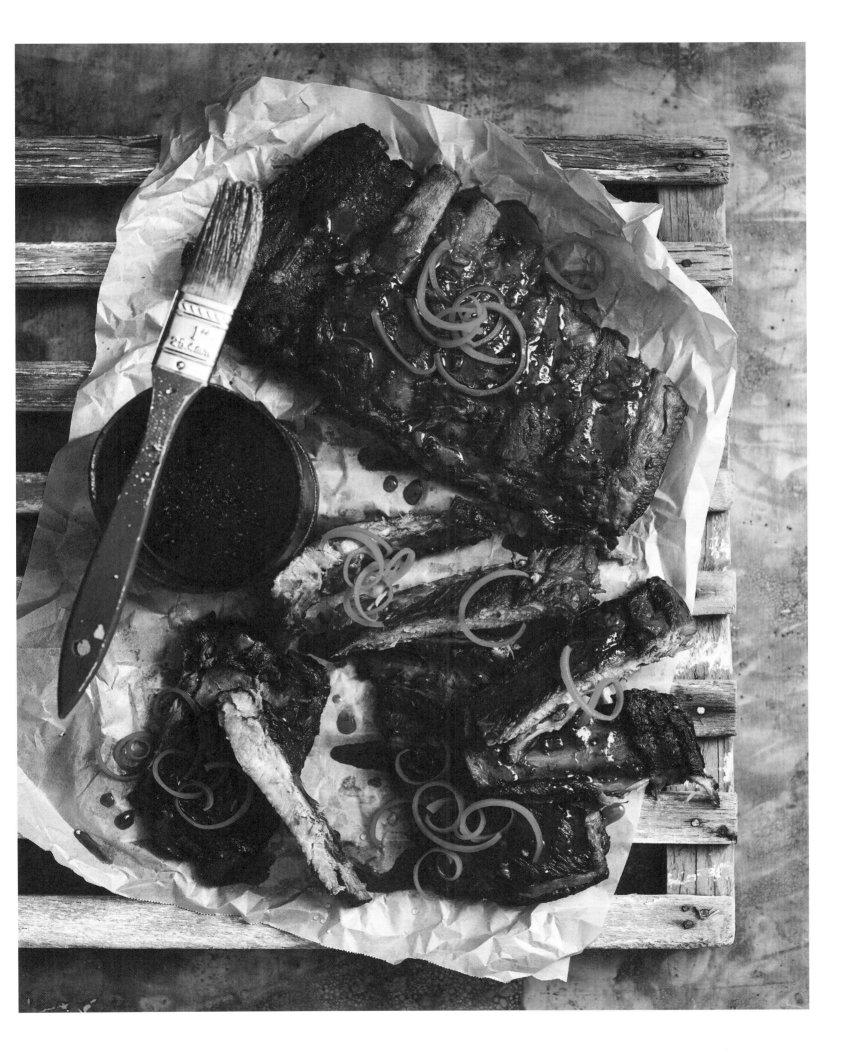

cranberry & red-wine glazed lamb chops

PREP TIME 5 MINUTES COOK TIME 6 HOURS 20 MINUTES SERVES 4

FIVE INGREDIENTS

2 tablespoons plain (all-purpose) flour

8 lamb forequarter chops (1.5kg)

¼ cup (80g) whole cranberry sauce

1 tablespoon wholegrain mustard

½ cup (125ml) dry red wine

STAPLES

sea salt flakes

freshly ground black pepper

2 tablespoons olive oil

1 Place flour in a large bowl; season.

2 Heat oil in a 5-litre (20-cup) slow cooker on 'sear' (HIGH) setting. Trim and discard excess fat from lamb. Coat lamb in flour mixture; shake off excess. Cook lamb, in batches, for 5 minutes on each side or until well browned. Remove from cooker.

3 Meanwhile, whisk cranberry sauce, mustard, wine and ¾ cup (180ml) water in a large jug until combined.

4 Place 4 lamb chops in slow cooker. Pour half the wine mixture over lamb; repeat with remaining lamb chops and wine mixture. Adjust setting to LOW; cook, covered, for 6 hours.

5 Remove lamb from slow cooker; cover to keep warm. Skim fat from surface of sauce; season to taste. Serve lamb with sauce.

MAKE IT SIX *Add 2 thickly sliced red onions in step 4.*

SERVE IT *with the basic mash or mushy peas and mint on page 66, if you like.*

STORE IT *Refrigerate in an airtight container for up to 3 days, or freeze for up to 3 months; thaw in the fridge.*

balsamic roast chicken

PREP TIME 5 MINUTES **COOK TIME** 6 HOURS 10 MINUTES **SERVES** 4

FIVE INGREDIENTS

4 cloves garlic

¼ cup fresh oregano leaves

2 tablespoons dijon mustard

1 tablespoon brown sugar

2kg (4lb) whole chicken

STAPLES

½ cup (125ml) balsamic vinegar

1 tablespoon olive oil

sea salt flakes

freshly ground black pepper

1 Coarsely chop garlic and half the oregano. Place garlic, chopped oregano, mustard, sugar, vinegar and oil in a 5-litre (20-cup) slow cooker; stir to combine.

2 Trim and discard excess fat from chicken cavity. Heat slow cooker on LOW. Place chicken in cooker; turn to coat in mixture. Cook, covered, for 6 hours.

3 Carefully remove chicken from slow cooker; cover to keep warm. Adjust setting to 'reduce' (HIGH). Skim and discard fat from surface of cooking liquid; bring to the boil. Boil, uncovered, for 10 minutes or until sauce is reduced to ½ cup.

4 Drizzle chicken with sauce and scatter with remaining oregano; season. Serve.

SERVE IT *with one of the salads on page 106 or vegie sides on page 26.*

SWAP IT *Use 2 tablespoons fresh thyme or lemon thyme leaves or 1 tablespoon finely chopped fresh rosemary instead of oregano, if preferred.*

five-spice caramel pork belly

PREP TIME 20 MINUTES **COOK TIME** 6 HOURS 45 MINUTES **SERVES** 6

FIVE INGREDIENTS

2kg (4lb) boneless pork belly

1 cup (220g) caster (superfine) sugar

1 cup (250ml) unsweetened coconut water

¾ cup (180ml) fish sauce

2 teaspoons chinese five spice

STAPLES

freshly ground black pepper

1 Remove pork rind; cut pork into 6cm (2½in) pieces. Place pork and 2 litres (8 cups) water in a large saucepan; bring to the boil over medium heat. Boil for 5 minutes, skimming impurities from surface; drain.

2 Meanwhile, combine sugar and ½ cup (125ml) water in a small saucepan; stir over high heat, without boiling, until sugar dissolves. Bring to the boil. Boil mixture, without stirring, until a deep golden caramel forms.

3 Heat a 5-litre (20-cup) slow cooker on LOW. Place pork, caramel, coconut water, fish sauce, five spice and 1 cup (250ml) water in cooker. Cook, covered, for 6 hours.

4 Remove lid. Adjust setting to HIGH; cook for a further 30 minutes. Skim fat from surface.

5 Transfer pork from slow cooker to a bowl with a slotted spoon. Strain liquid into a small saucepan. Bring to the boil; boil, uncovered, until reduced by half.

6 Serve pork with sauce; season with pepper.

MAKE IT SIX *Add 2 star anise or 3 crushed cloves garlic in step 3.*

SERVE IT *with the steamed ginger rice on page 192 and steamed asian greens on page 26.*

chorizo & chickpea stew

PREP TIME 5 MINUTES **COOK TIME** 7 HOURS 10 MINUTES **SERVES** 4

FIVE INGREDIENTS

2 x 400g (12½oz) cans chickpeas (garbanzo beans)

500g (1lb) cured chorizo

1 tablespoon harissa paste

500g (1lb) jar tomato pasta sauce

120g (4oz) baby spinach leaves

STAPLES

sea salt flakes

freshly ground black pepper

extra virgin olive oil

1 Preheat a 5-litre (20-cup) slow cooker on 'sear' (HIGH) setting.

2 Drain, then rinse chickpeas.

3 Cut chorizo into chunks; add to slow cooker. Cook, uncovered, turning, for 5 minutes or until browned lightly. Add harissa; cook for 30 seconds. Add tomato pasta sauce; bring to a simmer. Stir in chickpeas; season.

4 Adjust setting to LOW; cook, covered, for 7 hours or until sauce is reduced, rich and thickened.

5 Add spinach; stir until wilted. Drizzle with oil; season. Serve.

MAKE IT SIX *Add chopped garlic or rosemary in step 3 with the chickpeas.*

SERVE IT *with the grilled sourdough, garlic naan or cheddar toast on page 130, if you like.*

beef ribs with stout & caramelised onions

PREP TIME 5 MINUTES   **COOK TIME** 6 HOURS 45 MINUTES   **SERVES** 4

FIVE INGREDIENTS

8 beef short ribs (1.6kg)

2 cups (500ml) stout beer

280g (9oz) jar spicy caramelised onion

400g (12½oz) can diced tomatoes

3 fresh bay leaves

STAPLES

sea salt flakes

freshly ground black pepper

1   Preheat a 5-litre (20-cup) slow cooker on 'sear' (HIGH) setting. Cook ribs, in batches, fat-side down, for 5 minutes or until browned.

2   Add remaining ingredients to slow cooker; season with salt and pepper. Adjust setting to LOW; cook, covered, for 6 hours 30 minutes.

3   Transfer ribs to a tray or large ovenproof dish; cover to keep warm. Skim fat from sauce. Adjust setting to 'reduce' (HIGH). Pour cooking liquid into a large jug. Measure 3 cups liquid (see tip); return to slow cooker. Discard any remaining liquid in jug. Bring to a simmer; simmer, uncovered, for 10 minutes or until sauce is reduced and thickened. Discard bay leaves.

4   Season ribs to taste; serve with sauce. Scatter with extra fresh bay leaves, if you like.

tip   If you don't have enough liquid in step 3, add water to make 3 cups.

SERVE IT *with the basic mash or cheesy polenta on page 66, if you like.*

STORE IT *Refrigerate in an airtight container for up to 3 days, or freeze for up to 3 months; thaw in the fridge.*

apricot chicken

PREP TIME 10 MINUTES **COOK TIME** 6 HOURS **SERVES** 6

FIVE INGREDIENTS

45g (1½oz) packet cream of chicken simmer soup mix

1⅔ cups (410ml) apricot nectar

1 medium leek (350g)

6 chicken marylands (2.1kg)

¾ cup (75g) dried apricot halves

STAPLES

sea salt flakes

freshly ground black pepper

1 Place soup mix in a 5-litre (20-cup) slow cooker. Gradually whisk in nectar until smooth; season to taste.

2 Trim leek, reserving green top. Rinse leek well; slice thickly.

3 Remove and discard fat and skin from chicken. Heat slow cooker on LOW. Place chicken, leek and dried apricots in cooker; cook, covered, for 6 hours.

4 Meanwhile, rinse some of the reserved green leek top. Cut into long thin strips. Season chicken to taste; serve scattered with leek strips.

SERVE IT *with the almond pilaf or cauliflower rice on page 192 and the simple green salad on page 106, if you like.*

STORE IT *Refrigerate in an airtight container for up to 2 days, or freeze for up to 2 months; thaw in the fridge.*

braised beans & ham

PREP TIME 5 MINUTES **COOK TIME** 8 HOURS **SERVES** 6

FIVE INGREDIENTS

4 x 400g (12½oz) cans pinto beans

410g (13oz) can tomato puree

⅓ cup (75g) firmly packed brown sugar

2 tablespoons dijon mustard

1kg (2lb) smoked ham hock

STAPLES

sea salt flakes

freshly ground black pepper

1 Heat a 5-litre (20-cup) slow cooker on LOW. Drain, then rinse beans. Place beans, puree, sugar, mustard, ham hock and ½ cup (125ml) water in cooker; cook, covered, for 8 hours.

2 Remove ham hock from slow cooker; discard rind. Coarsely shred or slice ham; discard bone. Season to taste. Serve ham with bean mixture.

SWAP IT *Use wholegrain mustard instead of dijon, if preferred.*

SERVE IT *with the cheddar toast or grilled sourdough on page 130.*

STORE IT *Refrigerate in an airtight container for up to 3 days, or freeze for up to 3 months; thaw in the fridge.*

4 easy *bread sides*

1

GARLIC NAAN

prep + cook time 25 minutes **serves** 6

Preheat oven to 180°C/350°F. Place 4 plain naan breads on a baking-paper-lined oven tray; prick all over with a fork. Combine ⅓ cup extra virgin olive oil, 2 crushed cloves garlic and 2 tablespoons coarsely chopped fresh chives or coriander (cilantro) in a small bowl; season. Spread herb and garlic mixture evenly on bread. Bake for 15 minutes or until bread is golden and crisp.

2

GRILLED SOURDOUGH

prep + cook time 10 minutes **serves** 4

Cut 8 thin slices from a loaf of sourdough bread. Brush bread lightly with extra virgin olive oil; place on a heated oiled grill plate (or grill or barbecue) for 1 minute on each side or until lightly charred. Rub with a cut clove of garlic, if you like.

3

CHEDDAR TOASTS

prep + cook time 15 minutes **serves** 4

Preheat oven to 200°C/400°F. Place 8 slices sourdough on a baking-paper-lined oven tray; top with 150g (4½oz) sliced cheddar. Bake for 8 minutes or until cheddar melts. Sprinkle with freshly ground black pepper, if you like.

4

SIMPLE YOGHURT FLATBREAD

prep + cook time 20 minutes (+ standing) **makes** 4

Place 1 cup self-raising flour in a medium bowl; cut in ½ cup Greek-style yoghurt with a butter knife. Bring mixture together with your hands. Knead dough lightly until smooth. Stand for 5 minutes. Divide dough into four pieces; roll each piece on a floured surface to about a 20cm (8in) long oval. Heat 2 teaspoons olive oil in a medium frying pan over high heat. Cook one piece of dough at a time for 30 seconds on each side, or until puffy and golden, adding extra oil to pan each time. Scatter with flat-leaf parsley leaves, if you like.

bread sides

glazed chicken drumsticks

PREP TIME 5 MINUTES COOK TIME 7 HOURS 15 MINUTES SERVES 4

FIVE INGREDIENTS

3 cloves garlic

6cm (2½in) piece fresh ginger

½ cup (125ml) kecap manis

8 chicken drumsticks (1.2kg)

½ cup fresh mint leaves

1 Peel and thinly slice garlic. Peel and finely grate ginger. Add garlic, ginger, kecap manis and 2 cups (500ml) water to slow cooker. Add chicken in a single layer.

2 Heat slow cooker on LOW. Cook, covered, turning chicken half way through cooking time, for 7 hours or until chicken is very tender. Transfer chicken to a large plate or tray. Strain sauce; return to cooker.

3 Adjust setting to 'reduce' (HIGH); simmer sauce for 15 minutes or until reduced slightly. Serve chicken with sauce as a glaze; season. Scatter with mint leaves.

MAKE IT SIX *Add 2 teaspoons chinese five spice in step 1 or scatter with toasted sesame seeds to serve.*

SERVE IT *with the steamed asian greens on page 26 and steamed ginger rice on page 192.*

tuscan beef stew

PREP TIME 5 MINUTES **COOK TIME** 6 HOURS 15 MINUTES **SERVES** 4

FIVE INGREDIENTS

8 pieces beef osso buco (1.6kg)

6 anchovy fillets

400g (12½oz) can diced tomatoes

4 sprigs fresh rosemary

1 cup (120g) pitted green olives

STAPLES

1 tablespoon olive oil

¼ cup (60ml) balsamic vinegar

sea salt flakes

freshly ground black pepper

1 Trim excess fat from beef. Heat oil in 5-litre (20-cup) slow cooker on 'sear' (HIGH) setting. Cook beef, in batches, until browned on both sides; remove from cooker.

2 Add chopped anchovy to slow cooker; cook, stirring, for 1 minute or until fragrant. Stir in vinegar, canned tomatoes, 1¼ cups (310ml) water and rosemary. Adjust setting to LOW; cook, covered, for 6 hours. Stir in olives; season to taste.

3 Scatter stew with extra rosemary, if you like; serve.

SERVE IT *with the cheesy polenta on page 66 or almond gremolata on page 168, if you like.*

STORE IT *Refrigerate in an airtight container for up to 3 days, or freeze for up to 3 months; thaw in the fridge.*

shredded beef tacos

PREP TIME 10 MINUTES **COOK TIME** 6 HOURS **MAKES** 6

FIVE INGREDIENTS

1kg (2lb) piece beef chuck steak

30g (1oz) packet taco seasoning mix

1 baby cos (romaine) lettuce

12 mini flour tortillas (300g)

½ cup (120g) sour cream

STAPLES

sea salt flakes

freshly ground black pepper

1 Heat a 5-litre (20-cup) slow cooker on LOW. Rub beef with seasoning mix and place in cooker. Pour 1 cup (250ml) water over beef; cook, covered, for 6 hours.

2 Remove beef from slow cooker. When cool enough to handle, shred meat coarsely using two forks. Discard half the liquid from cooker. Season remaining liquid to taste.

3 Meanwhile, trim and wash lettuce. Shred lettuce or leave whole.

4 Warm tortillas following packet directions. Serve lettuce and beef in tortillas, topped with sour cream and drizzled with a little of the cooking liquid. Season; serve.

MAKE IT SIX *Add grated cheddar in step 4, if you like.*

SERVE IT *with the chunky guacamole on page 168.*

STORE IT *Refrigerate beef mixture at the end of step 2 in an airtight container for up to 3 days, or freeze for up to 3 months; thaw in the fridge.*

pot-roasted tarragon chicken

PREP TIME 20 MINUTES **COOK TIME** 7 HOURS **SERVES** 4

FIVE INGREDIENTS

2kg (4lb) whole chicken

2 bulbs garlic

2 medium lemons (280g)

500g (1lb) kipfler (fingerling) potatoes

2 tablespoons fresh tarragon leaves

STAPLES

1 tablespoon extra virgin olive oil

2 teaspoons sea salt flakes

1 teaspoon freshly ground black pepper

50g (1½oz) butter

1 Pat chicken dry with paper towel; tie legs together with kitchen string. Halve garlic crossways. Slice lemons into thirds. Scrub potatoes.

2 Preheat oil in a 5-litre (20-cup) slow cooker on 'sear' (HIGH) setting.

3 Transfer chicken to slow cooker; cook, turning, for 10 minutes or until browned all over. Transfer to a plate. Add garlic, cut-side down; cook for 5 minutes or until golden. Add lemon, flesh-side down; cook with garlic for a further 3 minutes. Return chicken to cooker. Add potatoes and tarragon; season with salt and pepper.

4 Adjust setting to LOW; cook for 6 hours 30 minutes or until chicken is cooked through. Remove chicken, garlic, lemon, potatoes and tarragon. Strain juices through a sieve; return to cooker.

5 Adjust setting to 'reduce' (HIGH). Squeeze garlic from 1 garlic bulb into juices in slow cooker. Bring to the boil; simmer, uncovered, for 10 minutes or until reduced and thickened.

6 Meanwhile, cut butter into small cubes; add to slow cooker. Blend garlic, butter and juices in cooker using a stick blender until a smooth sauce forms.

7 Serve chicken with remaining garlic, the lemon, potatoes, sauce and extra tarragon, if you like; season.

SERVE IT *with the lemony lettuce wedges on page 106 or minted greens on page 26, if you like.*

STORE IT *Refrigerate the chicken in an airtight container for up to 2 days. Recipe is not suitable to freeze.*

honey-soy lamb chops

PREP TIME 20 MINUTES **COOK TIME** 6 HOURS 15 MINUTES **SERVES** 4

FIVE INGREDIENTS

8 small lamb forequarter chops (1.6kg)

3 large red onions (900g)

¼ cup (60ml) salt-reduced soy sauce

¼ cup (90g) honey

100g (3oz) baby kale

STAPLES

¼ cup (60ml) olive oil

1 tablespoon red wine vinegar

sea salt flakes

freshly ground black pepper

1 Trim chops to remove excess fat. Cut 2 onions into thick wedges.

2 Combine soy sauce, honey and 1 tablespoon of the oil in a small jug.

3 Heat a 5-litre (20-cup) slow cooker on LOW. Place onion wedges in cooker; top with lamb and soy sauce mixture. Cook, covered, for 6 hours.

4 Remove lamb and onion from slow cooker; cover to keep warm. Skim fat from liquid. Adjust setting to 'reduce' (HIGH); cook liquid, uncovered, for 15 minutes or until slightly sticky. Strain sauce through a fine sieve into a medium jug.

5 To make salad, combine remaining oil and vinegar in a large bowl. Thinly slice remaining red onion. Add onion and kale to bowl with dressing; season and toss gently.

6 Serve lamb and onion with sauce and salad.

MAKE IT SIX *Add 1 crushed garlic clove in step 2.*

SERVE IT *with the sweet potato mash or mushy peas and mint on page 66, if you like.*

STORE IT *Refrigerate in an airtight container for up to 3 days, or freeze for up to 3 months; thaw in the fridge.*

piri piri chicken

PREP TIME 15 MINUTES **COOK TIME** 6 HOURS 15 MINUTES **SERVES** 4

FIVE INGREDIENTS

1.8kg (3¾lb) whole chicken

2 medium lemons (280g)

6 sprigs fresh thyme

⅔ cup (160ml) medium piri piri marinade

½ cup (150g) whole-egg mayonnaise

STAPLES

1 tablespoon olive oil

sea salt flakes

freshly ground black pepper

1 Pat chicken dry inside and out with paper towel. Cut 1 lemon into wedges. Place lemon wedges and 4 thyme sprigs inside cavity of chicken; secure cavity with a fine skewer.

2 Make a pocket under skin of breasts, drumsticks and thighs with your fingers. Using disposable gloves, rub ¼ cup of the marinade under skin. Tuck wing tips under; tie legs together with kitchen string. Rub another ⅓ cup marinade over chicken.

3 Heat oil in a 5-litre (20-cup) slow cooker on 'sear' (HIGH) setting. Cook chicken, turning, until browned all over.

4 Adjust setting to LOW; cook chicken, covered, for 6 hours.

5 Cut chicken into pieces. Cut remaining lemon into wedges. Swirl remaining piri piri marinade through mayonnaise.

6 Serve chicken topped with remaining thyme sprigs, with mayonnaise mixture and lemon wedges to the side; season.

SWAP IT *Use a piri piri marinade with your chosen heat level instead of medium, if preferred.*

SERVE IT *with the shake and bake wedges or corn cobs with parmesan and paprika on page 26, or the classic slaw or perfect potato salad on page 106, if you like.*

lamb chops with ratatouille

PREP TIME 10 MINUTES **COOK TIME** 6 HOURS 20 MINUTES **SERVES** 4

FIVE INGREDIENTS

4 lamb forequarter chops (1kg)

1 large eggplant (500g)

1 medium zucchini (120g)

1 medium yellow capsicum (bell pepper) (200g)

2 x 400g (12½oz) jars tomato basil pasta sauce

STAPLES

1 tablespoon olive oil

sea salt flakes

freshly ground black pepper

1 Trim and discard excess fat from lamb. Cut eggplant into 2.5cm (1in) pieces. Cut zucchini into pieces. Halve capsicum, remove seeds and membrane, then cut into pieces.

2 Heat oil in a 5-litre (20-cup) slow cooker on 'sear' (HIGH) setting. Season lamb with salt and pepper. Cook lamb, in batches, for 5 minutes on each side or until well browned. Return lamb to cooker.

3 Add eggplant, zucchini, capsicum and pasta sauce to slow cooker. Adjust setting to LOW; cook, covered, for 6 hours.

4 Serve lamb chops with ratatouille; season to taste.

MAKE IT SIX *Add 1 red onion, cut into thick wedges or 3 cloves crushed garlic in step 3.*

SERVE IT *topped with the broccoli pesto on page 168 or with the cheesy polenta on page 66, if you like.*

Under 10 hours

pork laksa

PREP TIME 15 MINUTES **COOK TIME** 8 HOURS 10 MINUTES **SERVES** 4

FIVE INGREDIENTS

1kg (2lb) pork rashers

1 bunch green onions (scallions)

230g (7oz) jar laksa paste

2 x 270ml cans coconut milk

250g (8oz) dried rice vermicelli noodles

STAPLES

freshly ground black pepper

1 Remove and discard top layer of skin and fat from each pork rasher. Cut pork rashers into 3cm (1¼in) pieces. Transfer to a 5-litre (20-cup) slow cooker.

2 Finely chop white part of green onions. Add white part to slow cooker; refrigerate green tops for serving. Add laksa paste, 1 can of coconut milk and 1.5 litres (6 cups) water to cooker; stir to combine.

3 Heat slow cooker on LOW. Cook pork, covered, for 8 hours or until tender. Skim and discard fat from surface.

4 Adjust setting to HIGH. Add remaining coconut milk; cook, covered, for a further 10 minutes.

5 Meanwhile, place noodles in a heatproof bowl; cover with boiling water. Stand for 5 minutes; drain. Cut green onion tops into long thin strips. If onion doesn't curl, add to a bowl of iced water and stand for a few minutes.

6 Divide soup mixture, pork and noodles among bowls. Top with green onion curls; season with pepper. Serve.

MAKE IT SIX *Top with finely chopped fresh red chillies, mint leaves or bean sprouts, or serve with lime wedges to the side.*

SWAP IT *Use the same weight of skinless chicken thighs instead of pork rashers, if preferred.*

red-wine-braised beef short ribs

PREP TIME 5 MINUTES **COOK TIME** 9 HOURS 20 MINUTES **SERVES** 4

FIVE INGREDIENTS

8 small cloves garlic

8 beef short ribs (1.6kg)

100g (3oz) tomato paste

3 cups (750ml) red wine

8 sprigs fresh thyme

STAPLES

1 tablespoon extra virgin olive oil

1 teaspoon sea salt flakes

2 teaspoons freshly ground black pepper

1 Coarsely chop garlic.

2 Heat oil in a 5-litre (20-cup) slow cooker on 'sear' (HIGH) setting. Add beef in batches; cook, turning, for 5 minutes on each side or until browned all over. Transfer ribs to a large plate or tray.

3 Add garlic to slow cooker; cook for 1 minute. Add tomato paste; cook, stirring, for 2 minutes. Add wine; bring to the boil, then cook, uncovered, for 10 minutes or until reduced slightly. Return ribs to cooker; scatter with 6 sprigs of thyme. Season with salt and pepper.

4 Adjust setting to LOW; cook, covered, for 8 hours 30 minutes.

5 Carefully transfer ribs to an oven tray. Skim any excess fat from top of sauce. Adjust setting to 'reduce' (HIGH); simmer sauce for 15 minutes or until thickened.

6 Meanwhile, heat oven grill (broiler) on high; grill ribs until browned.

7 Top ribs with sauce and remaining thyme; season. Serve.

MAKE IT SIX *Add 1 large red onion, cut into wedges, to the slow cooker with the garlic in step 3.*

SERVE IT *with the grilled sourdough on page 130 or basic mash on page 66, if you like.*

fetta, spinach & lemon rolled lamb

PREP TIME 30 MINUTES **COOK TIME** 8 HOURS 15 MINUTES **SERVES** 6

FIVE INGREDIENTS

180g (5½oz) marinated persian fetta in oil

100g (3oz) baby spinach leaves

1 medium lemon (140g)

1.5kg (3lb) boneless lamb leg

250g (8oz) cherry truss tomatoes

STAPLES

¼ cup (60ml) balsamic vinegar

sea salt flakes

freshly ground black pepper

1 tablespoon extra virgin olive oil

1 Drain fetta; reserving 2 tablespoons of the oil. Coarsely chop three-quarters of the spinach. Finely grate half the lemon to yield 2 teaspoons rind; reserve lemon.

2 Combine fetta, chopped spinach, grated rind and 1 tablespoon of the vinegar in a bowl; season to taste.

3 Place lamb on a chopping board, fat-side down. Open out lamb; slice through thickest part horizontally, without cutting all the way through. Open out the flap to form one large even piece. Spread fetta mixture over lamb. Roll lamb up to enclose the filling, securing with kitchen string at 2cm (¾in) intervals. Season lamb with salt and pepper.

4 Heat half the reserved oil in a 5-litre (20-cup) slow cooker on 'sear' (HIGH) setting. Cook lamb, turning, until browned all over.

5 Combine remaining reserved oil and 1½ tablespoons of the vinegar in a small bowl; brush over lamb. Adjust setting to LOW; cook, covered, for 8 hours.

6 Place remaining spinach and halved tomatoes in a medium bowl. Drizzle with olive oil and remaining vinegar; season.

7 Use a zesting tool to remove rind from other half of the lemon; cut the lemon into wedges.

8 Top lamb with lemon rind strips; season. Serve with spinach salad and lemon wedges.

MAKE IT SIX *Add kalamata olives or sliced cucumber to the spinach salad in step 6, if you like.*

SERVE IT *with the grilled sourdough or garlic naan on page 130, if you like.*

simple beef stroganoff

PREP TIME 15 MINUTES **COOK TIME** 9 HOURS 45 MINUTES **SERVES** 4

FIVE INGREDIENTS

1.5kg (3lb) beef chuck steak

12 red shallots (300g)

300g (9½oz) small swiss brown mushrooms

1 tablespoon sweet paprika

⅓ cup (80g) crème fraîche

STAPLES

1 tablespoon olive oil

sea salt flakes

freshly ground black pepper

1 Trim beef to remove excess fat; cut into 4cm (1½in) pieces.

2 Heat oil in a 5-litre (20-cup) slow cooker on 'sear' (HIGH) setting. Cook beef, in batches, turning, for 5 minutes or until well browned.

3 Peel shallots. Add shallots, mushrooms (halve some mushrooms, if you like) and paprika; cook, stirring, for 2 minutes or until fragrant. Add ½ cup (125ml) water. Adjust setting to LOW; cook, covered, for 9 hours 30 minutes.

4 Stir in crème fraîche; cook for a further 1 minute or until heated through. Season to taste. Serve drizzled with extra crème fraîche and sprinkled with extra paprika, if you like.

SWAP IT *Use button mushrooms instead of swiss brown mushrooms, if you like. Replace beef with diced pork.*

SERVE IT *with the mashed potato on page 66, if you like.*

hoisin pork buns

PREP TIME 15 MINUTES **COOK TIME** 10 HOURS **MAKES** 24

FIVE INGREDIENTS

1.8kg (3¾lb) boneless pork shoulder

½ cup (125ml) hoisin sauce

¼ cup (60ml) salt-reduced soy sauce

24 gwa pao buns (720g)

4 baby cucumbers (qukes) (200g)

STAPLES

1 tablespoon olive oil

2 tablespoons rice wine vinegar

freshly ground black pepper

1 Remove and discard rind and excess fat from pork. Heat oil in a 5-litre (20-cup) slow cooker on 'sear' (HIGH) setting. Cook pork, turning, for 5 minutes or until well browned.

2 Add ⅓ cup of the hoisin sauce, the soy sauce, vinegar and ⅓ cup (80ml) water to slow cooker. Adjust setting to LOW; cook, covered, for 9 hours 45 minutes.

3 Carefully remove pork from slow cooker; shred meat coarsely using two forks. Skim any fat from cooking liquid. Return shredded pork to cooker; stir to coat with sauce. Cover to keep warm.

4 Heat buns following packet directions.

5 Cut cucumbers into thin wedges.

6 Fill buns with pork mixture and cucumber. Combine remaining hoisin sauce with 2 tablespoons water in a bowl. Serve buns drizzled with hoisin mixture. Season with pepper.

SWAP IT *Use white wine vinegar instead of rice wine vinegar.*

SERVE IT *Omit the buns and serve with the steamed ginger rice on page 192 and steamed asian greens on page 26.*

STORE IT *Refrigerate pork mixture at the end of step 3 in an airtight container for up to 3 days, or freeze for up to 3 months; thaw in the fridge.*

saucy italian roast beef

PREP TIME 15 MINUTES **COOK TIME** 8 HOURS 10 MINUTES **SERVES** 6

FIVE INGREDIENTS

2 medium onions (300g)

300g (9½oz) button mushrooms

1.5kg (3lb) piece fresh beef silverside

2 x 500g (1lb) jars tomato, onion & roast garlic pasta sauce

300g (9½oz) spiral pasta

STAPLES

1 tablespoon extra virgin olive oil

sea salt flakes

freshly ground black pepper

1½ tablespoons balsamic vinegar

1 Peel and halve onions, leaving roots intact. Cut each half into three wedges. Trim mushroom stems.

2 Heat oil in a 5-litre (20-cup) slow cooker on 'sear' (HIGH) setting. Add beef; cook, turning, for 2 minutes on each side or until browned all over.

3 Add onion, mushrooms and pasta sauce to slow cooker. Add ¼ cup (60ml) water to each jar of pasta sauce; screw on lids and shake to remove remaining sauce. Pour water mixture over beef; season with salt and pepper.

4 Adjust setting to LOW; cook, covered, for 7 hours 30 minutes. Add pasta, stirring to ensure it is covered with sauce. Cook, covered, for a further 30 minutes or until pasta is tender. Stir in balsamic vinegar; season to taste.

5 Remove beef; slice thinly. Serve with onion, mushroom and tomato pasta mixture; season with pepper.

SERVE IT *topped with the broccoli pesto on page 168 or the simple green salad on page 106, if you like.*

STORE IT *Refrigerate in an airtight container for up to 3 days, or freeze for up to 3 months; thaw in the fridge.*

pork belly with fennel

PREP TIME 20 MINUTES **COOK TIME** 8 HOURS 50 MINUTES **SERVES** 4

FIVE INGREDIENTS

2 teaspoons fennel seeds

1kg (2lb) piece boneless pork belly

4 medium fennel bulbs (1.2kg)

3 cups (750ml) apple cider

4 medium red apples (600g)

STAPLES

sea salt flakes

¼ cup (60ml) extra virgin olive oil

2 tablespoons apple cider vinegar

freshly ground black pepper

1 Coarsely crush fennel seeds with a mortar and pestle or spice grinder; mix with 1 tablespoon salt flakes. Pat pork dry with paper towel; score skin at 1cm (½in) intervals. Rub fennel salt over pork.

2 Cut 2 fennel bulbs into quarters; reserve fronds.

3 Heat 2 tablespoons of the oil in a 5-litre (20-cup) slow cooker on 'sear' (HIGH) setting. Cook pork on each side for 5 minutes or until browned. Transfer to a plate.

4 Add quartered fennel to slow cooker; cook for 5 minutes or until golden. Add pork and apple cider. Adjust setting to HIGH; cook, covered, for 7 hours.

5 Core 3 apples and cut into quarters. Add apple to slow cooker; cook, covered, for a further 1 hour or until pork is very tender.

6 Preheat an oven grill (broiler) on high. Remove pork from slow cooker, rind-side up, to a shallow roasting pan or oven tray. Grill pork for 20 minutes or until browned and crisp.

7 Place fennel and apple on a plate; cover to keep warm. Skim fat from liquid in slow cooker. Adjust setting to 'reduce' (HIGH); simmer sauce, uncovered, for 15 minutes or until thickened. Season to taste.

8 Thinly slice remaining fennel and apple using a V-slicer or mandoline; transfer to a bowl. Add remaining oil and the vinegar; season, then toss to combine.

9 Serve pork with the braised fennel and apple, drizzled with pan juices; scatter with reserved fennel fronds. Serve with the fennel and apple salad. Season with pepper, if you like.

PREP IT *The pork can be prepared up to the end of step 1 a day ahead and refrigerated, uncovered.*

SERVE IT *with the sweet potato mash on page 66, if you like.*

tex mex beef & sweet potato

PREP TIME 15 MINUTES **COOK TIME** 8 HOURS **SERVES** 4

FIVE INGREDIENTS

800g (1½lb) beef chuck steak

2 medium orange sweet potatoes (800g)

1 bunch coriander (cilantro)

400g (12½oz) can diced tomatoes with garlic & olive oil

35g (1oz) packet mexican chilli spice mix

STAPLES

sea salt flakes

freshly ground black pepper

1 Trim beef of excess fat; cut into 5cm (2in) pieces. Cut unpeeled sweet potatoes into 5cm (2in) pieces. Wash coriander well; chop roots and stems and reserve leaves.

2 Heat a 5-litre (20-cup) slow cooker on LOW. Place beef, sweet potato, chopped coriander, canned tomatoes, spice mix and ½ cup (125ml) water in cooker; cook, covered, for 8 hours.

3 Season to taste; scatter with reserved coriander leaves. Serve.

SERVE IT *with the chunky guacamole or spiced lime yoghurt on page 168, the simple green salad on page 130, or the simple yoghurt flatbread on page 130.*

STORE IT *Refrigerate in an airtight container for up to 3 days, or freeze for up to 3 months; thaw in the fridge.*

soy-braised pork

PREP TIME 15 MINUTES **COOK TIME** 8 HOURS 10 MINUTES **SERVES** 4

FIVE INGREDIENTS

1kg (2lb) piece pork scotch fillet (neck) (see tip)

2 star anise

½ cup (125ml) salt-reduced soy sauce

½ cup (125ml) chinese cooking wine (shao hsing)

⅓ cup (75g) firmly packed brown sugar

1 Tie pork with kitchen string at 2.5cm (1in) intervals. Heat a 5-litre (20-cup) slow cooker on LOW. Place all ingredients in cooker; cook, covered, for 8 hours.

2 Remove pork from slow cooker; cover to keep warm. Adjust setting to 'reduce' (HIGH); simmer, uncovered, for 10 minutes or until sauce thickens slightly.

3 Remove string. Discard star anise. Serve sliced pork with sauce.

tip Ask the butcher to tie the pork for you to save time.

MAKE IT SIX *Add 2 cinnamon sticks, or 1 tablespoon finely grated ginger, or 2 cloves crushed garlic in step 1.*

SERVE IT *with the steamed ginger rice on page 192 and steamed asian greens on page 26, if you like.*

red-wine-braised beef

PREP TIME 10 MINUTES **COOK TIME** 8 HOURS 15 MINUTES **SERVES** 4

FIVE INGREDIENTS

4 x 250g (8oz) beef cheeks

3 fresh bay leaves

1½ cups (375ml) dry red wine

¼ cup (70g) tomato paste

500g (1lb) exotic mushroom mix

STAPLES

2 tablespoons olive oil

sea salt flakes

1 teaspoon cracked black pepper

1 Heat oil in a 5-litre (20-cup) slow cooker on 'sear' (HIGH) setting. Season beef with salt; cook for 5 minutes on each side or until well browned. Remove from cooker.

2 Add bay leaves, pepper, wine and tomato paste; bring to the boil, stirring. Stir in ½ cup (125ml) water. Return beef to slow cooker.

3 Adjust setting to LOW; cook, covered, for 7 hours. Stir in mushrooms; cook, covered, for a further 1 hour or until mushrooms are tender.

4 Discard bay leaves; season to taste. Serve beef with pan juices.

MAKE IT SIX *Add a finely chopped onion, carrot or trimmed celery stalk in step 2, if you like.*

SERVE IT *with one of the mashes or polenta on page 66 and the minted greens on page 26, if you like.*

4 easy *toppers*

1

BROCCOLI PESTO

prep + cook time 15 minutes **serves** 4

Cook 100g (3oz) chopped broccoli in a small saucepan of boiling water for 2 minutes; drain. Refresh in cold water; drain well. Process broccoli, 1 clove crushed garlic, 1½ tablespoons toasted pine nuts, 1½ tablespoons grated parmesan and 1½ tablespoons coarsely chopped basil until finely chopped. With motor operating, gradually pour in ¼ cup extra virgin olive oil; process until combined. Season to taste. Scatter with extra pine nuts and basil leaves, if you like.

2

ALMOND GREMOLATA

prep time 10 minutes **makes** 1 cup

Coarsely chop ½ cup roasted natural almonds. Combine almonds in a medium bowl with 1 crushed clove garlic, 1 tablespoon grated lemon rind and ½ cup chopped fresh flat-leaf parsley.

3

SPICED LIME YOGHURT

prep time 5 minutes **makes** ½ cup

Stir ½ cup Greek-style yoghurt, 1 crushed clove garlic, 1 tablespoon lime juice and a pinch cayenne pepper in a small bowl; season to taste. Top with finely grated lime rind and a little extra cayenne pepper, if you like.

4

CHUNKY GUACAMOLE

prep time 15 minutes **serves** 4

Combine 1 coarsely mashed large avocado, 1 thinly sliced green onion (scallion), 2 tablespoons chopped fresh coriander (cilantro) leaves, 100g (3oz) halved or quartered grape tomatoes and 2 tablespoons lime juice in a small bowl. Season to taste. Top with extra coriander leaves, if you like.

toppers

chipotle beef chilli

PREP TIME 15 MINUTES **COOK TIME** 9 HOURS **SERVES** 4

FIVE INGREDIENTS

1.5kg (3lb) beef chuck steak

2 medium capsicums (bell peppers) (400g)

400g (12½oz) can red kidney beans

400g (12½oz) can diced tomatoes

2 tablespoons chipotle in adobo sauce

STAPLES

sea salt flakes

freshly ground black pepper

1 Trim beef of excess fat; cut into 3cm (1¼in) pieces. Halve capsicums, remove seeds and membranes, then slice thickly. Drain, then rinse beans.

2 Heat a 5-litre (20-cup) slow cooker on LOW. Transfer beef, capsicum and beans to cooker. Add ½ cup (125ml) water, canned tomatoes and chipotle; cook, covered, for 9 hours.

3 Season chilli to taste; serve.

SWAP IT *Use pork instead of beef, if preferred.*

SERVE IT *with the guacamole or spiced lime yoghurt on page 168, or with the yoghurt flatbreads on page 130, if you like.*

STORE IT *Refrigerate in an airtight container for up to 3 days, or freeze for up to 3 months; thaw in the fridge.*

lamb shanks with tomato & kale

PREP TIME 15 MINUTES **COOK TIME** 8 HOURS 30 MINUTES **SERVES** 4

FIVE INGREDIENTS

3 trimmed stalks celery (300g)

4 small french-trimmed lamb shanks (800g)

½ cup (125ml) dry white wine

410g (13oz) can tomato puree

100g (3oz) baby kale

STAPLES

¼ cup (60ml) olive oil

sea salt flakes

freshly ground black pepper

1 tablespoon red wine vinegar

1 Chop 2 celery stalks.

2 Heat 1 tablespoon of the oil in a 5-litre (20-cup) slow cooker on 'sear' (HIGH) setting. Season lamb with salt and pepper. Cook lamb, in batches, for 15 minutes or until well browned. Remove from cooker.

3 Adjust setting to 'sear' (MEDIUM); cook chopped celery, stirring, for 5 minutes or until softened.

4 Add wine; bring to the boil. Stir in tomato puree. Return lamb to slow cooker. Adjust setting to LOW; cook, covered, for 8 hours. Season.

5 To make dressing, combine remaining oil and the vinegar in a large bowl; season to taste. Use a vegetable peeler or mandoline to shave long strips from remaining celery. Place shaved celery and kale in bowl with the dressing; toss well.

6 Serve lamb shanks with sauce and kale salad; season with pepper.

MAKE IT SIX *Top with crumbled fetta before serving.*

SERVE IT *with the cheesy polenta or basic mash on page 66, if you like.*

STORE IT *Refrigerate in an airtight container for up to 2 days, or freeze at the end of step 4 for up to 3 months; thaw in the fridge.*

balsamic beef pot roast

PREP TIME 10 MINUTES **COOK TIME** 8 HOURS 50 MINUTES **SERVES** 8

FIVE INGREDIENTS

2.2kg (4½lb) piece beef blade roast

10 small cloves garlic

3 medium red onions (500g)

1 celery heart

1 dried bouquet garni

STAPLES

2 tablespoons extra virgin olive oil

1 cup (250ml) balsamic vinegar

sea salt flakes

freshly ground black pepper

1 Heat oil in a 5-litre (20-cup) slow cooker on 'sear' (HIGH) setting.

2 Make 10 small incisions in top of beef, about 4cm (1½in) deep. Peel garlic; insert into incisions. Halve onions, leaving roots intact. Trim then quarter celery lengthways; reserve small leaves for serving.

3 Place beef in slow cooker, fat-side down. Cook for 5 minutes or until browned and fat is rendered; transfer beef to a large plate or tray. Add onion, cut-side down, to slow cooker; cook for 3 minutes or until browned. Return beef to cooker along with any collected juices. Add celery, bouquet garni, balsamic vinegar and 1 cup (250ml) water. Season with salt and pepper.

4 Adjust setting to LOW; cook, covered, for 8 hours 30 minutes. Transfer beef carefully to a large plate; add onion and celery. Skim fat from liquid in slow cooker.

5 Adjust setting to 'reduce' (HIGH); bring to the boil, then simmer, uncovered, for 10 minutes or until sauce is reduced by half and thickened. Season to taste.

6 Thickly slice beef; serve with onions, celery and sauce, topped with reserved celery leaves.

SERVE IT *with the minted greens and the shake and bake wedges on page 26, or the basic mash on page 66, if you like.*

STORE IT *Refrigerate beef and sauce in an airtight container for up to 3 days, or freeze for up to 3 months; thaw in the fridge.*

thai coconut pork curry

PREP TIME 15 MINUTES **COOK TIME** 9 HOURS 30 MINUTES **SERVES** 4

FIVE INGREDIENTS

½ bunch fresh coriander (cilantro)

1kg (2lb) pork scotch fillet

¼ cup (80g) thai red curry paste

500g (1lb) frozen thai stir-fry vegetables

165ml can coconut milk

STAPLES

1 tablespoon olive oil

sea salt flakes

freshly ground black pepper

1 Wash coriander thoroughly. Separate roots, stems and leaves; finely chop enough of the roots and stems to yield ¼ cup. Reserve the leaves for serving.

2 Cut pork into 4cm (1½in) pieces.

3 Heat oil in a 5-litre (20-cup) slow cooker on 'sear' (HIGH) setting. Cook pork, in batches, turning, for 5 minutes or until well browned.

4 Add curry paste; cook, stirring, for 1 minute or until fragrant. Add chopped coriander and ½ cup (125ml) water. Adjust setting to LOW; cook, covered, for 9 hours.

5 Add frozen vegetables and coconut milk. Adjust setting to 'reduce' (HIGH); cook, uncovered, for 15 minutes or until vegetables are hot and sauce thickens. Season to taste.

6 Scatter curry with reserved coriander leaves; serve.

MAKE IT SIX *Add a squeeze of lime juice before serving and serve with lime wedges.*

SWAP IT *Use scotch fillet steaks with the bone in if available; leave them whole as the bone adds flavour. Or you can use diced beef such as chuck or blade steak, if you prefer.*

massaman beef curry

PREP TIME 10 MINUTES **COOK TIME** 9 HOURS 45 MINUTES **SERVES** 4

FIVE INGREDIENTS

800g (1½lb) beef chuck steak

1 medium sweet potato (400g)

⅓ cup (100g) massaman curry paste

400ml can coconut milk

3 limes (200g)

STAPLES

2 tablespoons olive oil

sea salt flakes

freshly ground black pepper

1 Trim excess fat from beef; cut into 5cm (2in) pieces. Peel and cut sweet potato into 5cm (2in) pieces.

2 Heat oil in a 5-litre (20-cup) slow cooker on 'sear' (HIGH) setting. Cook beef, in batches, turning, for 5 minutes or until well browned.

3 Add curry paste and sweet potato; stir for 2 minutes or until fragrant. Add coconut milk and ½ cup (125ml) water. Adjust setting to LOW; cook, covered, for 9 hours 30 minutes.

4 Use a zesting tool to remove the rind from 1 lime. Juice 2 limes. Cut remaining lime into wedges for serving. Add 1½ tablespoons lime juice to curry. Season to taste.

5 Scatter curry with lime rind; serve with lime wedges.

MAKE IT SIX *Add fish sauce to taste with the lime juice in step 4.*

SWAP IT *Replace beef chuck steak with diced beef or blade steak. Replace sweet potato with potato.*

chicken cacciatore

PREP TIME 5 MINUTES **COOK TIME** 8 HOURS 10 MINUTES **SERVES** 4

FIVE INGREDIENTS

4 chicken marylands (1.4kg) or 8 thigh cutlets (1.6kg)

2 large onions (400g)

1 large green capsicum (bell pepper) (350g)

400g (12½oz) arrabbiata pasta sauce

¾ cup (120g) pitted kalamata olives

STAPLES

1 tablespoon olive oil

sea salt flakes

freshly ground black pepper

1 Heat oil in a 5-litre (20-cup) slow cooker on 'sear' (HIGH) setting. Cook chicken, skin-side down, for 10 minutes or until golden.

2 Meanwhile, quarter onions. Halve capsicum, remove seeds and membrane, then cut into wedges.

3 Add onion and pasta sauce to slow cooker. Pour ½ cup (125ml) water into sauce jar; screw lid on and shake to remove remaining sauce. Pour over chicken. Adjust setting to LOW; cook, covered, for 7 hours 30 minutes or until chicken is tender.

4 Add capsicum and olives to slow cooker; cook, covered, for a further 30 minutes. Season to taste; serve.

SERVE IT *with the cheesy polenta on page 66 or the cauliflower 'rice' on page 192, if you like.*

STORE IT *Refrigerate in an airtight container for up to 2 days, or freeze for up to 3 months; thaw in the fridge.*

beer-braised beef brisket

PREP TIME 5 MINUTES **COOK TIME** 8 HOURS 40 MINUTES (+ STANDING) **SERVES** 6

FIVE INGREDIENTS

4 cloves garlic

100g (3oz) smoked streaky bacon slices

1.25kg (2½lb) piece beef brisket

1½ teaspoons smoked paprika

1⅓ cups (330ml) lager beer

STAPLES

sea salt flakes

freshly ground black pepper

2 teaspoons olive oil

1 Peel and crush garlic. Chop bacon. Season brisket with salt and pepper. Heat oil in a 5-litre (20-cup) slow cooker on 'sear' (HIGH) setting. Cook brisket, fat-side down, for 10 minutes or until golden.

2 Add garlic, bacon, paprika, beer and 2 cups (500ml) water to slow cooker; bring to a simmer, uncovered. Adjust setting to LOW; cook, covered, for 8 hours or until very tender. Transfer brisket carefully to a shallow roasting pan or oven tray, fat-side up.

3 Preheat oven grill (broiler) on high. Grill brisket for 10 minutes or until lightly browned. Cover with foil; stand for 10 minutes.

4 Skim fat from sauce. Strain sauce; discard solids. Return strained sauce to slow cooker. Adjust setting to 'reduce' (HIGH); simmer for 20 minutes or until thickened slightly.

5 Season brisket; slice and serve with sauce.

MAKE IT SIX *Add finely chopped fresh rosemary with the garlic in step 2.*

SERVE IT *with the classic coleslaw or perfect potato salad on page 106. Alternatively, serve as a filling in your favourite bread rolls.*

lamb madras

PREP TIME 5 MINUTES **COOK TIME** 8 HOURS 20 MINUTES **SERVES** 4

FIVE INGREDIENTS

800g (1½lb) diced lamb

2 medium onions (300g)

⅓ cup (100g) madras curry paste

100g (3oz) baby spinach leaves

100g (3oz) packet pappadums

STAPLES

1 tablespoon olive oil

sea salt flakes

freshly ground black pepper

1 Heat oil in a 5-litre (20-cup) slow cooker on 'sear' (HIGH) setting. Cook lamb, stirring, for 15 minutes or until well browned.

2 Peel and thinly slice onions. Add onion to slow cooker; cook, stirring, for 1 minute or until fragrant.

3 Add curry paste; cook, stirring, for 1 minute. Stir in ½ cup (125ml) water. Adjust setting to LOW; cook, covered, for 8 hours.

4 Stir half the spinach into curry until wilted. Season to taste.

5 Meanwhile, prepare pappadums following packet directions. Scatter curry with remaining spinach; serve with pappadums.

MAKE IT SIX *Add 1 tablespoon grated fresh ginger with the curry paste in step 3.*

SWAP IT *Use beef instead of lamb.*

SERVE IT *with the spiced lime yoghurt on page 168 and almond pilaf on page 192, if you like.*

pork vindaloo

PREP TIME 15 MINUTES **COOK TIME** 8 HOURS **SERVES** 6

FIVE INGREDIENTS

1.2kg (2½lb) pork scotch fillet (neck)

2 medium red onions (340g)

400g (12½oz) can diced tomatoes

½ cup (150g) vindaloo curry paste

20 fresh curry leaves

STAPLES

1 tablespoon apple cider vinegar

2 tablespoons vegetable oil

sea salt flakes

freshly ground black pepper

1 Cut pork into 3cm (1¼in) pieces; discard any excess fat. Cut onions into wedges.

2 Heat a 5-litre (20-cup) slow cooker on LOW. Place pork, onion, canned tomatoes, curry paste, vinegar, 8 curry leaves and ¾ cup (180ml) water in cooker; cook, covered, for 8 hours. Season to taste.

3 Close to serving, heat oil in a small saucepan on the stove. Carefully add remaining curry leaves (oil will bubble fiercely); fry for a few seconds until crisp. Remove from pan with a slotted spoon; drain on paper towel.

4 Serve curry topped with fried curry leaves.

SERVE IT *with the almond pilaf on page 192 or garlic naan on page 130, topped with the spiced lime yoghurt on page 168, if you like.*

STORE IT *Refrigerate in an airtight container for up to 3 days, or freeze for up to 3 months; thaw in the fridge.*

lamb wraps

PREP TIME 5 MINUTES **COOK TIME** 9 HOURS 50 MINUTES **SERVES** 6

FIVE INGREDIENTS

1.8kg (3¾lb) lamb shoulder with bone

¼ cup (30g) za'atar

6 large pitta bread (570g)

60g (2oz) rocket (arugula) leaves

¾ cup (180ml) tzatziki

STAPLES

2 tablespoons olive oil

sea salt flakes

freshly ground black pepper

1 Rub lamb all over with 2 tablespoons of the za'atar.

2 Heat oil in a 5-litre (20-cup) slow cooker on 'sear' (HIGH) setting. Cook lamb, turning, for 5 minutes or until well browned. Add ⅓ cup (80ml) water. Adjust setting to LOW; cook, covered, for 9 hours 45 minutes.

3 Carefully remove lamb from slow cooker. Shred meat coarsely using two forks; discard bones and cooking liquid.

4 Warm bread following packet directions. Top pitta bread with lamb, rocket and tzatziki; sprinkle with remaining za'atar and season to taste. Roll wraps to enclose filling; serve.

MAKE IT SIX *Add sliced tomato to the wraps in step 4, if you like.*

SWAP IT *Use boneless pork shoulder instead of lamb.*

STORE IT *Refrigerate lamb at the end of step 3 in an airtight container for up to 3 days. Recipe is not suitable to freeze.*

spicy italian sausage, fennel & tomato ragu

PREP TIME 10 MINUTES **COOK TIME** 8 HOURS 40 MINUTES **SERVES** 4

FIVE INGREDIENTS

2 medium fennel bulbs (600g)

12 Italian-style pork and veal sausages (850g)

½ cup (125ml) dry white wine

2 x 400g (12½oz) cans diced tomatoes with basil & oregano

¼ cup (20g) grated parmesan

STAPLES

1 tablespoon olive oil

sea salt flakes

freshly ground black pepper

1 Trim fennel bulbs, reserving fronds; cut into quarters. Heat half the oil in a 5-litre (20-cup) slow cooker on 'sear' (HIGH) setting. Cook sausages, turning occasionally, for 8 minutes or until well browned; remove from cooker.

2 Heat remaining oil in slow cooker; add fennel; cook, stirring, for 5 minutes or until softened and golden. Return sausages to cooker; add wine and canned tomatoes. Adjust setting to LOW; cook, covered, for 8 hours. Skim fat from sauce.

3 Adjust setting to 'reduce' (HIGH); simmer, uncovered, for 20 minutes or until sauce thickens slightly. Season to taste.

4 Top ragù with parmesan and reserved fennel fronds; serve.

SERVE IT *with the grilled sourdough or cheddar toast on page 130, or the cheesy polenta on page 66.*

STORE IT *Refrigerate in an airtight container for up to 3 days, or freeze for up to 3 months; thaw in the fridge.*

4 easy 'grain' sides

1

ALMOND PILAF

prep + cook time 30 minutes **serves** 4

Melt 20g (¾oz) butter in a medium saucepan; cook 1 crushed clove garlic, stirring, until fragrant. Add 1 cup basmati rice; cook, stirring, for 1 minute. Add 1 cup chicken stock and 1 cup water; bring to the boil. Reduce heat to low; cook, covered, for 20 minutes or until rice is just tender. Remove from heat; fluff rice with fork. Stir in ¼ cup coarsely chopped fresh flat-leaf parsley and ¼ cup toasted flaked natural almonds.

2

CAULIFLOWER 'RICE'

prep + cook time 15 minutes **serves** 4

Coarsely chop 750g (1½lb) cauliflower with stems. Process cauliflower using pulse button until resembling rice grains. Heat 2 tablespoons olive oil in a wok over medium heat. Add 2 crushed cloves garlic and 2 teaspoons finely grated fresh ginger (optional); stir for 1 minute or until fragrant. Add chopped cauliflower; stir occasionally for 4 minutes or until softened. Season to taste; scatter with chopped fresh flat-leaf parsley.

3

STEAMED GINGER RICE

prep + cook time 20 minutes (+ standing) **serves** 4

Heat 1 tablespoon olive oil in a medium saucepan; cook 6 thinly sliced green onions (scallions), stirring, until softened. Add 2½ teaspoons finely grated fresh ginger and 1 cup jasmine rice; stir to coat in oil. Add 2 cups chicken stock; bring to the boil. Reduce heat; simmer, covered, over low heat, for 15 minutes. Stand, covered, for 5 minutes; fluff with a fork. Stir in 2 tablespoons finely chopped fresh coriander (cilantro); season to taste. Scatter with extra coriander leaves, if you like.

4

LEMON PISTACHIO COUSCOUS

prep + cook time 15 minutes (+ standing) **serves** 4

Combine 1 cup couscous, ¾ cup boiling water, 2 teaspoons finely grated lemon rind and ¼ cup lemon juice in a heatproof bowl. Cover; stand for 5 minutes or until liquid is absorbed. Fluff with a fork. Meanwhile, dry-fry ½ cup pistachios in a heated small frying pan until fragrant; chop coarsely. Heat 2 teaspoons olive oil in same pan; cook 1 finely chopped small red onion, stirring, until softened. Stir pistachios, onion mixture and ½ cup shredded fresh mint into couscous; season to taste.

'grain' sides

ginger-mango chutney lamb

PREP TIME 15 MINUTES **COOK TIME** 9 HOURS 30 MINUTES **SERVES** 8

FIVE INGREDIENTS

2kg (4lb) lamb shoulder with bone

354g (11½oz) jar mango & ginger chutney

½ cup (125ml) sriracha sauce

8 greek yiros wraps (760g) or naan bread

½ cup (140g) Greek-style yoghurt

STAPLES

2 tablespoons white wine vinegar

2 tablespoons olive oil

1 teaspoon sea salt flakes

1 teaspoon freshly ground black pepper

1 Trim lamb of any excess fat. Place ¾ cup of the chutney, the sriracha and vinegar in a small bowl; stir well.

2 Heat half the oil in a 5-litre (20-cup) slow cooker on 'sear' (HIGH) setting. Add lamb; cook, turning, for 10 minutes or until browned all over. Season with salt and pepper.

3 Add sauce mixture to slow cooker; turn lamb to coat. Adjust setting to LOW; cook, covered, for 9 hours or until lamb is tender. Carefully transfer lamb to a large plate or tray. Skim excess fat from surface of sauce.

4 Adjust setting to 'reduce' (HIGH); bring sauce to the boil. Simmer for 10 minutes or until sauce is reduced and thickened. Shred lamb from bone; return meat to sauce.

5 Heat a chargrill pan over high heat. Brush wraps with remaining oil; grill for 1 minute on each side or until grill marks appear and wraps are warmed through. Swirl remaining chutney through yoghurt.

6 Serve lamb with wraps and yoghurt mixture, and extra sriracha, if you like.

MAKE IT SIX *Add salad leaves or sliced cucumber to the wraps, if you like.*

STORE IT *Refrigerate lamb at the end of step 4 in an airtight container for up to 3 days, or freeze for up to 3 months; thaw in the fridge.*

chinese chicken hotpot

PREP TIME 20 MINUTES **COOK TIME** 8 HOURS 10 MINUTES **SERVES** 6

FIVE INGREDIENTS

1.8kg (3¾lb) whole chicken

5cm (2in) piece fresh ginger

2 cups (500ml) chinese cooking wine (shao hsing)

⅔ cup (80ml) oyster sauce

2 bunches baby buk choy

STAPLES

freshly ground black pepper

1 Pat chicken dry inside and out with paper towel. Peel ginger; cut into matchsticks.

2 Heat a 5-litre (20-cup) slow cooker on LOW. Combine 2 litres (8 cups) water, cooking wine, half the oyster sauce and the ginger in cooker. Add chicken; cook, covered, for 8 hours.

3 Remove chicken; cover to keep warm. Strain broth through a fine sieve into a large bowl; discard solids. Halve buk choy lengthways; wash well.

4 Return broth to slow cooker; season with pepper. Add buk choy to cooker. Adjust setting to HIGH; cook, covered, for 5 minutes or until just tender.

5 Cut chicken into six pieces. Serve chicken, broth and buk choy drizzled with remaining oyster sauce; season with pepper.

MAKE IT SIX *Add 2 star anise or 4 cloves bruised garlic in step 2.*

SERVE IT *with the steamed ginger rice on page 192, if you like.*

STORE IT *Refrigerate in an airtight container for up to 2 days. Recipe is not suitable to freeze.*

picadillo beef

PREP TIME 15 MINUTES **COOK TIME** 9 HOURS 20 MINUTES **SERVES** 4

FIVE INGREDIENTS

1.5kg (3lb) gravy beef

½ bunch fresh coriander (cilantro)

1 tablespoon ground cumin

2 x 400g (12½oz) cans diced tomatoes with basil & oregano

1 cup (180g) pitted green sicilian olives

STAPLES

1 tablespoon olive oil

sea salt flakes

freshly ground black pepper

1 Cut beef into 3cm (1¼in) pieces. Wash coriander well; separate roots, stems and leaves. Finely chop enough coriander roots and stems to yield ¼ cup; reserve leaves for serving.

2 Heat oil in a 5-litre (20-cup) slow cooker on 'sear' (HIGH) setting. Cook beef, in batches, turning, for 5 minutes or until well browned.

3 Add cumin and chopped coriander to slow cooker; cook, stirring, for 1 minute or until fragrant. Add canned tomatoes and ½ cup (125ml) water. Adjust setting to LOW; cook, covered, for 9 hours.

4 Stir in olives and reserved coriander leaves; season to taste. Serve.

SWAP IT *Replace beef with diced pork, if preferred.*

SERVE IT *with the cauliflower rice on page 192 or the simple green salad on page 106.*

lamb shank korma

PREP TIME 5 MINUTES **COOK TIME** 8 HOURS 10 MINUTES **SERVES** 6

FIVE INGREDIENTS

6 small french-trimmed lamb shanks (1.5kg)

400g (12½oz) can diced tomatoes

300ml pouring cream

280g (9oz) jar korma curry paste

2 cups (240g) frozen peas

STAPLES

sea salt flakes

freshly ground black pepper

1 Heat a 5-litre (20-cup) slow cooker on LOW. Combine lamb, canned tomatoes, 1 cup of the cream and the curry paste in cooker. Refrigerate remaining cream for serving. Cook, covered, for 8 hours.

2 Add peas to slow cooker; cook, covered, for 10 minutes or until heated through.

3 Spoon over remaining cream; season. Serve.

SERVE IT *with the garlic naan on page 130 or the almond pilaf on page 192, if you like.*

STORE IT *Refrigerate in an airtight container for up to 3 days, or freeze for up to 3 months; thaw in the fridge.*

chilli con carne

PREP TIME 5 MINUTES **COOK TIME** 8 HOURS 50 MINUTES **SERVES** 6

FIVE INGREDIENTS

750g (1½lb) minced (ground) beef

2 x 25g (¾oz) packets burrito spice mix

2 x 400g (12½oz) cans diced tomatoes

2 x 400g (12½oz) cans kidney beans

175g (5½oz) corn chips

STAPLES

1 tablespoon olive oil

sea salt flakes

freshly ground black pepper

1 Heat oil in a 5-litre (20-cup) slow cooker on 'sear' (HIGH) setting. Cook beef, stirring, for 15 minutes or until browned. Add spice mix; cook, stirring, for 1 minute. Stir in canned tomatoes and 1 cup (250ml) water. Adjust setting to LOW; cook, covered, for 8 hours.

2 Drain, then rinse beans. Add beans to slow cooker. Adjust setting to HIGH; cook, covered, for 30 minutes or until hot. Season.

3 Serve chilli con carne with corn chips.

MAKE IT SIX *Add 1 finely chopped large onion in step 1, or serve with grated cheddar.*

SERVE IT *with chunky guacamole or spiced lime yoghurt on page 168.*

sticky glazed beef ribs

PREP TIME 5 MINUTES **COOK TIME** 8 HOURS 10 MINUTES **SERVES** 4

FIVE INGREDIENTS

½ cup (140g) tomato sauce (ketchup)

½ cup (140g) sweet chilli sauce

⅓ cup (80ml) soy sauce

¼ cup (90g) honey

8 beef short ribs (2kg)

STAPLES

sea salt flakes

freshly ground black pepper

1 Heat a 5-litre (20-cup) slow cooker on LOW. Combine sauces, honey and ⅓ cup (80ml) water in cooker. Add beef; turn to coat in mixture. Cook, covered, for 8 hours. Carefully remove beef from cooker; cover to keep warm.

2 Transfer the sauce to a saucepan; bring to the boil. Boil, skimming fat from surface, for 10 minutes or until sauce reduces to 2 cups.

3 Serve beef with sauce; season.

MAKE IT SIX *Use ⅓ cup bourbon instead of water in step 1.*

SERVE IT *with the perfect potato salad on page 106, or the shake and bake wedges or corn cobs on page 26, if you like.*

STORE IT *Refrigerate in an airtight container for up to 3 days, or freeze for up to 3 months; thaw in the fridge.*

pork in ginger beer

PREP TIME 10 MINUTES **COOK TIME** 8 HOURS **SERVES** 6

FIVE INGREDIENTS

6 green onions (scallions)

1.5kg (3lb) piece pork scotch fillet (neck)

1½ teaspoons ground ginger

1½ cups (375ml) ginger beer

¼ cup (55g) firmly packed dark brown sugar

STAPLES

2 tablespoons olive oil

sea salt flakes

freshly ground black pepper

1 Cut white part of green onions and half the green tops into 4cm (1½in) lengths. Refrigerate green onion lengths and remaining green onion tops.

2 Heat half the oil in a 5-litre (20-cup) slow cooker on 'sear' (HIGH) setting. Season pork; add to cooker. Cook, turning occasionally, for 20 minutes or until well browned. Remove pork from cooker.

3 Heat remaining oil in slow cooker; cook white lengths of green onion, stirring, for 5 minutes. Add ground ginger; cook, stirring, for 1 minute or until fragrant. Stir in ginger beer, sugar and ⅓ cup (80ml) water. Return pork to cooker. Adjust setting to LOW; cook, covered, for 7 hours 15 minutes.

4 Carefully remove pork from slow cooker to a plate; cover to keep warm. Adjust setting to 'reduce' (HIGH). Add green lengths of green onion; simmer, uncovered, for 20 minutes or until sauce thickens slightly. Season to taste.

5 Meanwhile, cut remaining green onion tops into long thin strips. Place in a bowl of iced water to curl.

6 Slice pork thickly. Serve pork drizzled with some of the cooking liquid and scattered with the curled green onion tops. Season.

MAKE IT SIX *Add 2 teaspoons fennel seeds or 1 stem fresh rosemary with ginger beer in step 3.*

SERVE IT *with the sweet potato mash or mushy peas and mint on page 66.*

mexican pull-apart pork

PREP TIME 15 MINUTES COOK TIME 8 HOURS SERVES 6

FIVE INGREDIENTS

3 chipotle in adobo sauce

375g (12oz) jar chunky mild tomato salsa

1 cup (280g) barbecue sauce

1kg (2lb) boneless pork shoulder

½ cup (120g) sour cream

STAPLES

sea salt flakes

freshly ground black pepper

1 Finely chop chipotle; reserve 2 teaspoons of the adobo sauce. Heat a 5-litre (20-cup) slow cooker on LOW. Combine salsa, barbecue sauce and two-thirds of the chipotle in cooker. Add pork and turn to coat in mixture; cook, covered, for 8 hours.

2 Carefully remove pork from slow cooker; shred meat using two forks. Return shredded pork to cooker; stir gently. Season to taste.

3 Combine sour cream with remaining chipotle and reserved adobo sauce; serve with the pork.

MAKE IT SIX *Serve with shredded lettuce or lime wedges, or as a filling for taco shells, if you like.*

SERVE IT *with the simple yoghurt flatbread on page 130, if you like.*

STORE IT *Refrigerate in an airtight container at the end of step 2 for up to 3 days, or freeze for up to 3 months; thaw in the fridge. Reheat, then continue with step 3 just before serving.*

Slow-cooker sweets

classic brownie

PREP TIME 20 MINUTES **COOK TIME** 3 HOURS 10 MINUTES (+ COOLING) **MAKES** 24

FIVE INGREDIENTS

300g (9½oz) dark (semi-sweet) chocolate

6 large eggs

3 cups (660g) firmly packed brown sugar

1¾ cups (260g) plain (all-purpose) flour

1 cup (100g) roasted walnuts

STAPLES

250g (8oz) unsalted butter

1 Line a rectangular slow cooker with two layers of baking paper; do not preheat.

2 Finely chop 200g (6½oz) of the chocolate; cut remaining 100g (3oz) into chunks. Crack eggs into a bowl; beat lightly.

3 Microwave chopped butter in a large microwave-safe bowl until melted; stir in sugar. Microwave for a further 1 minute or until very hot. Stir in the finely chopped chocolate until chocolate melts. Whisk in egg in two batches; stir in flour.

4 Pour batter into lined slow cooker. Smooth surface to remove any air bubbles. Scatter with reserved chocolate chunks and coarsely chopped walnuts.

5 Heat slow cooker on LOW. Cover slow cooker insert with a clean tea towel, then replace cooker lid; cook for 3 hours. Turn off cooker; leave brownie to cool for 20 minutes in cooker, covered.

6 Transfer brownie to a cutting board; cut into 24 pieces.

SWAP IT *Use macadamias, pecans or almonds instead of walnuts, if preferred.*

STORE IT *Refrigerate in an airtight container for up to 4 days; warm in a microwave before serving, if you like.*

pumpkin pudding pie

PREP TIME 25 MINUTES **COOK TIME** 4 HOURS 10 MINUTES (+ STANDING & REFRIGERATION) **SERVES** 10

FIVE INGREDIENTS

500g (1lb) cream cheese

800g (1½lb) butternut pumpkin

1¼ cups (275g) caster (superfine) sugar

1½ teaspoons mixed spice

3 large eggs

STAPLES

100g (3oz) butter

1 Remove cream cheese and butter from fridge to soften.

2 Peel pumpkin; chop coarsely. Transfer to a microwave-safe bowl; cover with two layers of plastic wrap. Microwave for 10 minutes or until pumpkin is soft. Drain on paper towel.

3 Meanwhile, preheat slow cooker on HIGH.

4 Grease and line base and side of a 20cm (8in) springform cake pan with baking paper. Cut a 1m (39in) long piece of foil. Wrap foil around outside of pan, joining ends together on top to make a 'handle' so it looks like a basket, to assist with removing pan from the slow cooker. Place pan inside slow cooker.

5 Beat half the softened cream cheese, 1 cup of the sugar and 1 teaspoon of the mixed spice in a bowl with an electric mixer until well combined and smooth. Add one egg at a time, beating well after each addition. Process pumpkin in a food processor until smooth. Add pumpkin to cream cheese mixture; whisk to combine well.

6 Pour mixture into lined pan; place in slow cooker. Cover slow cooker insert with a clean tea towel, then replace cooker lid. Cook, covered, for 4 hours. Turn cooker off; remove lid. Stand pudding inside cooker for 1 hour, covered with the tea towel. Using the foil handle, remove pudding from slow cooker; cover and refrigerate pudding for 4 hours or until cold.

7 Before serving, beat softened butter, remaining cream cheese, remaining sugar and ¼ teaspoon of the mixed spice in a medium bowl with an electric mixer until light and fluffy. Spread icing over chilled pumpkin pie; sprinkle with remaining mixed spice.

MAKE IT SIX *Scatter with coarsely chopped pecans or walnuts; this will add a textural contrast to the smooth and creamy pie.*

STORE IT *Refrigerate, covered, for up to 3 days. This recipe is not suitable to freeze.*

berry cobbler

PREP TIME 20 MINUTES **COOK TIME** 1 HOUR 40 MINUTES **SERVES** 6

FIVE INGREDIENTS

1 large navel orange (425g)

1kg (2lb) frozen mixed berries

1 tablespoon wheaten cornflour (cornstarch) (see tip)

⅓ cup (55g) pure icing (confectioners') sugar

500g (1lb) packaged scone mix

1 Preheat slow cooker on HIGH.

2 Remove rind from orange in long, thin strips using a zesting tool; refrigerate until serving. Juice orange. Place slightly thawed berries, cornflour and ¼ cup of the icing sugar in slow cooker; mix well. Pour over orange juice; cook, covered, for 35 minutes.

3 Meanwhile, mix scone mix and 1 cup (250ml) water together until combined. Turn dough onto a work surface dusted lightly with extra cornflour. Using cornflour-dusted hands, flatten dough to 3cm (1¼in) thick. Cut into 4cm (1½in) rounds using a scone cutter. Re-roll scraps and repeat. Place dough rounds on top of berry mixture. Cover slow cooker insert with a clean tea towel, then replace cooker lid. Cook, covered, for a further 1 hour or until scone topping is cooked through.

4 Dust with remaining icing sugar; top with orange rind.

tip Wheaten cornflour will give a better texture to the sauce; you can use regular cornflour, if preferred.

MAKE IT SIX *Serve with thick cream, custard or vanilla ice-cream.*

STORE IT *Cobbler is best eaten straight away. This recipe is not suitable to freeze.*

sticky spiced macadamia & treacle cake

PREP TIME 30 MINUTES **COOK TIME** 3 HOURS (+ STANDING) **SERVES** 12

FIVE INGREDIENTS

1¼ cups (450g) treacle

3 large eggs

2 cups (300g) self-raising flour

1 teaspoon mixed spice

200g (6½oz) honey macadamias

STAPLES

240g (7½oz) butter

1 tablespoon red wine vinegar

¼ teaspoon sea salt flakes

1 Preheat a 5-litre (20-cup) slow cooker on HIGH. Place a wire rack in the base of the cooker.

2 Grease a deep 20cm (8in) round cake pan; line base and side with baking paper.

3 Beat 200g (6½oz) of the butter and ¾ cup of the treacle in a bowl with an electric mixer for 3 minutes or until light and fluffy. Add 1 egg at a time, beating after each addition until smooth (mixture may appear split).

4 Sift flour and mixed spice into a bowl; add half the flour mixture to butter mixture. Beat on low speed for 30 seconds or until well combined. Scrape down side of bowl; add remaining flour mixture. Beat on low speed for 1 minute or until smooth; do not overwork.

5 Add remaining butter and treacle to a small saucepan; stir over medium heat until boiling. Simmer for 5 minutes. Stir in vinegar, salt and macadamias. Pour mixture over base of lined cake pan.

6 Drop large spoonfuls of cake batter over caramel in pan. Carefully spread evenly over base; some caramel will come up the side. Place pan on rack in slow cooker. Cover with lid. Cook for 2 hours 45 minutes or until a skewer inserted into the centre comes out clean. Stand cake, uncovered, in cooker for 15 minutes.

7 Turn cake onto a plate; serve warm.

MAKE IT SIX *Serve with vanilla ice-cream, if you like.*

SWAP IT *Use honey instead of treacle, if preferred. Use ground cinnamon or ginger instead of the mixed spice.*

chocolate-hazelnut coffee scrolls

PREP TIME 25 MINUTES **COOK TIME** 2 HOURS 40 MINUTES (+ COOLING) **MAKES** 8

FIVE INGREDIENTS

4 cups (600g) self-raising flour

1½ tablespoons instant coffee granules

1½ cups (500g) chocolate-hazelnut spread

1 cup (220g) firmly packed brown sugar

1 large egg

STAPLES

100g (3oz) butter

½ teaspoon sea salt flakes

1 Preheat slow cooker on HIGH. Line insert with baking paper.

2 Dice butter.

3 Place flour, 1 tablespoon of the coffee and the salt in a large bowl of an electric mixer fitted with a dough hook attachment. Place ¼ cup of the chocolate-hazelnut spread, ½ cup of the sugar and the egg in a jug; whisk to combine. Add egg mixture and ⅓ cup (80ml) water to flour mixture; beat until it comes together into a smooth dough. Add diced butter slowly and beat well until incorporated and dough is smooth, shiny and elastic.

4 Transfer dough to a lightly floured surface; roll out to a 30cm x 40cm (12in x 16in) rectangle. Spread evenly with remaining chocolate-hazelnut spread. Roll up from the short side to form a log; cut dough into eight even rounds. Arrange rounds, cut-side up, in lined slow cooker insert. Cover insert with a clean tea towel, then replace cooker lid; cook for 2 hours 30 minutes or until dough is cooked through. Remove lid. Cool in cooker for 15 minutes, covered with the tea towel.

5 Just before serving, place remaining sugar, coffee and 1 tablespoon water in a small saucepan. Stir over medium heat until sugar dissolves. Cool slightly; drizzle over scrolls.

6 Transfer scrolls to a wire rack; serve immediately.

SWAP IT *Use vanilla extract instead of coffee granules. Add 1 teaspoon in the dough in step 3 and 1 teaspoon in the syrup in step 5.*

MAKE IT SIX *Serve with thick cream.*

STORE IT *Scrolls are best eaten straight away. This recipe is not suitable to freeze.*

mandarin & almond pudding

PREP TIME 35 MINUTES **COOK TIME** 5 HOURS (+ STANDING) **SERVES** 8

FIVE INGREDIENTS

6 small mandarins (600g)

4 eggs

1⅔ cup (370g) caster (superfine) sugar

1⅓ cups (160g) almond meal

⅔ cup (100g) self-raising flour

1 Heat a 5-litre (20-cup) slow cooker on HIGH. Place 4 washed and unpeeled mandarins in cooker; cover with hot water. Cook, covered, for 2 hours. Reserve 1 cup of the cooking water.

2 Trim ends from cooked mandarins; discard. Halve mandarins; remove and discard seeds. Process mandarins, including rind, until mixture is pulpy.

3 Grease a 2-litre (8-cup) pudding steamer.

4 Beat eggs and ⅔ cup of the sugar in a bowl with an electric mixer until thick and creamy. Fold in almond meal, sifted flour and mandarin pulp. Spoon mixture into steamer.

5 Place a sheet of baking paper on a sheet of foil; fold a 5cm (2in) pleat longways through the centre. Cover steamer with pleated baking paper and foil, paper-side down (this allows the pudding to expand during steaming; secure with kitchen string or lid.

6 Place steamer in slow cooker with enough boiling water to come halfway up side of steamer. Cook, covered, on HIGH for 3 hours, replenishing cooker with boiling water as necessary to maintain level. Stand pudding for 5 minutes, then turn onto a plate.

7 Meanwhile, to make mandarin syrup, peel remaining 2 mandarins. Cut rind into long thin strips. Keep fruit for another use. Combine reserved cooking water and remaining sugar in a small saucepan. Stir over low heat until sugar dissolves. Bring to the boil; boil, uncovered, for 5 minutes or until syrup is thickened. Remove from heat; stir in rind. Cool to room temperature.

8 Serve warm pudding with mandarin syrup drizzled on top.

MAKE IT SIX *Serve with cream, custard or ice-cream.*

STORE IT *Refrigerate pudding and syrup in separate airtight containers for up to 3 days. Pudding can be frozen for up to 3 months; thaw in the fridge.*

chocolate-hazelnut cheesecake

PREP TIME 30 MINUTES **COOK TIME** 2 HOURS (+ STANDING & REFRIGERATION) **SERVES** 10

FIVE INGREDIENTS

500g (1lb) cream cheese

250g (8oz) Delta Cream chocolate biscuits

½ cup (110g) caster (superfine) sugar

750g (1½lb) jar chocolate-hazelnut spread

3 eggs

STAPLES

80g (2½oz) butter

1 Grease a 20cm (8in) springform pan; line base and side with baking paper. Preheat a 5.5-litre (22-cup) slow cooker on HIGH. Make sure the pan fits in the slow cooker insert without touching the side; remove pan. Place a wire rack in the slow cooker insert. If you don't have a rack that will fit, tear off 1m (39in) foil; scrunch together to form a level 'rack' in the slow cooker.

2 Cut cream cheese into cubes; leave to soften at room temperature for 20 minutes. Microwave chopped butter in a microwave-safe bowl until melted.

3 Process biscuits until fine crumbs form. Add butter; process until combined. Press into base of lined pan; smooth surface with a spoon. Place in freezer for 5 minutes while preparing filling.

4 Meanwhile, process cream cheese and sugar in clean food processor until smooth and combined. Add 1½ cups (500g) of the chocolate spread; process again until combined. With motor operating, add 1 egg at a time; process until combined.

5 Add 1 cup (250ml) water to slow cooker. Pour batter into pan; place on rack or crumpled foil. Cover slow cooker insert with a clean tea towel, then replace cooker lid, tucking over the tea towel to wrap the lid.

6 Cook, covered, on HIGH for 2 hours. Turn slow cooker off; stand cheesecake inside covered cooker for 1 hour. Remove cheesecake; refrigerate until 30 minutes before serving.

7 Combine remaining chocolate-hazelnut spread with ⅓ cup (80ml) boiling water in a heatproof bowl; whisk until smooth. Add more water, if needed, for a thinner sauce.

8 Serve cheesecake drizzled with sauce.

MAKE IT SIX *Top with toasted hazelnuts before serving.*

STORE IT *Refrigerate cheesecake and sauce in separate airtight containers for up to 3 days. Recipe is not suitable to freeze.*

pecan pie

PREP TIME 20 MINUTES **COOK TIME** 1 HOUR 50 MINUTES **SERVES** 6

FIVE INGREDIENTS

1 sheet frozen shortcrust pastry (50g)

⅔ cup (230g) golden syrup

2 eggs

2 tablespoons plain (all-purpose) flour

2 cups (240g) pecans

STAPLES

50g (1½oz) butter

1 Remove pastry sheet from freezer to thaw.

2 Preheat slow cooker on HIGH. Grease a 20cm (8in) loose-based tart tin with a little extra butter. Line tin with pastry; trim excess pastry, leaving about 1cm (½in) overhang. Prick pastry with a fork; freeze while preparing the filling.

3 Melt butter in a microwave or small saucepan over medium heat. Whisk syrup, eggs, flour and melted butter in a jug; stir in pecans. Pour pecan mixture into pastry case, spreading filling evenly. Place tin in slow cooker. Cover slow cooker insert with a clean tea towel, then replace cooker lid. Cook, covered, for 1 hour 45 minutes.

4 Remove pie from slow cooker; cool slightly. Serve pie drizzled with extra golden syrup, if you like.

MAKE IT SIX *Serve with vanilla ice-cream or thick cream.*

STORE IT *Refrigerate in an airtight container for up to 4 days; serve cold or warm.*

golden syrup dumplings

PREP TIME 15 MINUTES COOK TIME 1 HOUR SERVES 4

FIVE INGREDIENTS

1 medium lemon (140g)

¾ cup (165g) caster (superfine) sugar

⅔ cup (160ml) golden syrup

1½ cups (225g) self-raising flour

2 eggs

STAPLES

110g (3½oz) butter

1 Preheat slow cooker on HIGH.

2 Remove half the rind from the lemon with a zesting tool. Remove remaining rind in wide strips and cut off any white pith. Coarsely chop butter.

3 Place 1½ cups (375ml) water in slow cooker; add 40g (1½oz) of the butter, half the lemon rind, the sugar and ½ cup of the golden syrup. Stir until sugar dissolves; bring to a simmer. Add wide strips of rind.

4 Sift flour into a bowl. Add remaining butter; rub into flour using your fingertips until it resembles fine bread crumbs. Make a well in the centre. Whisk eggs and 1 tablespoon water in a small bowl. Add egg mixture to flour mixture; stir using a flat-bladed knife to form a soft dough. Divide dough into 12 balls. Arrange dumplings on top of sauce mixture. Cover slow cooker insert with a clean tea towel, then replace cooker lid; cook for 50 minutes.

5 Top dumplings and sauce with remaining lemon rind; drizzle with remaining golden syrup. Serve immediately.

MAKE IT SIX *Serve with thick cream.*

STORE IT *Dumplings are best eaten straight away. This recipe is not suitable to freeze.*

pineapple coconut cake

PREP TIME 30 MINUTES **COOK TIME** 6 HOURS (+ COOLING) **SERVES** 8

FIVE INGREDIENTS

440g (14oz) can pineapple slices in syrup

400ml can coconut cream

1¼ cups (275g) caster (superfine) sugar

2 eggs

1½ cups (225g) self-raising flour

STAPLES

125g (4oz) butter

1 Chop butter into cubes; leave at room temperature to soften.

2 Preheat a 5.5-litre (22-cup) slow cooker on HIGH.

3 Grease a deep 20cm (8in) round cake pan; line base and side with baking paper.

4 Drain pineapple, reserving ⅔ cup of the syrup. Pat seven pineapple slices dry with paper towel; arrange over base of lined pan. Without shaking coconut cream can, open can and spoon off 1 cup of the thickest coconut cream into a jug; refrigerate until serving. Reserve ½ cup of remaining coconut cream.

5 Beat softened butter and ¾ cup of the sugar in a bowl with an electric mixer until light and fluffy. Add 1 egg at a time, beating well after each addition. Fold through sifted flour and the reserved ½ cup coconut cream until just combined.

6 Spoon batter into pan, tapping on the bench to remove air bubbles. Smooth surface with the back of the spoon. Cut a 1m (39in) long piece of foil. Wrap foil around outside of pan, joining ends together on top to make a 'handle' so it looks like a basket, to assist with removing the pan from the slow cooker. Place pan inside slow cooker. Cover slow cooker insert with a clean tea towel, then replace cooker lid. Cook for 6 hours or until a skewer inserted into the centre comes out clean. Using the foil handle, remove the pan from the slow cooker; cool cake in pan for 20 minutes.

7 Meanwhile, to make syrup, place remaining sugar and reserved pineapple syrup in clean slow cooker insert. Adjust setting to 'sear' (HIGH). Stir until sugar is dissolved. Bring to the boil; simmer for 10 minutes or until syrupy. (Or use a small saucepan on the stovetop.)

8 Run a flat-bladed knife around edge of pan; carefully turn cake onto a plate. Just before serving, whisk refrigerated thick coconut cream in a small bowl with an electric mixer until thick. Drizzle syrup over cake; serve with whipped coconut cream.

MAKE IT SIX *Add finely grated lime rind to the cake batter in step 5, then add julienned lime rind to the syrup in step 7.*

STORE IT *Refrigerate cake in an airtight container for up to 2 days; reheat in a microwave to serve.*

Glossary

ALMONDS, FLAKED paper-thin slices.

ANCHOVIES small oily fish. Anchovy fillets are preserved and packed in oil or salt in small cans or jars, and are strong in flavour. Fresh anchovies are much milder in flavour.

BASIL, SWEET the most common type of basil is sweet basil; used extensively in Italian dishes and one of the main ingredients in pesto.

BAY LEAVES aromatic leaves from the bay tree available fresh or dried; adds a strong, slightly peppery flavour.

BEANS

cannellini a small white bean similar in appearance and flavour to other white beans (great northern, navy or haricot), all of which can be substituted for the other. Available dried or canned.

four-bean a combination of butter beans, chickpeas (garbanzo beans), red kidney beans and baby lima beans.

green also known as french or string beans, this long thin fresh bean is consumed in its entirety once cooked.

kidney medium-sized red bean, slightly floury in texture, yet sweet in flavour.

mexe pinto beans combined with a hint of chilli and spices.

pinto an orange-pink bean with rust-coloured specks that grows across Latin America and the American South-West; commonly used fresh or canned in many dishes, especially Mexican refried beans.

BEEF

blade taken from the shoulder; isn't as tender as other cuts of beef, so it needs slow-roasting to achieve best results.

cheeks the cheek muscle of a cow. It's a very tough and lean cut of meat and is most often used for braising or slow cooking to produce a tender result.

chuck from the neck and shoulder of the cow; tends to be chewy but flavourful and inexpensive. A good cut for stewing or braising.

corned silverside also known as topside roast; sold vacuum-sealed in brine.

gravy beef also known as beef shin or shank, cut from the lower shin.

minced also known as ground beef.

osso buco literally meaning 'bone with a hole', osso buco is cut from the shin of the hind leg. It is also known as knuckle.

sausages seasoned and spiced minced (ground) beef mixed with cereal and packed into casings. Also known as snags or bangers.

short ribs cut from the rib section; usually larger, more tender and meatier than pork spare ribs.

silverside also called topside roast; the actual cut used for making corned beef.

BEETROOT (BEETS) also known as red beets; firm, round root vegetable.

BRANDY a general term for a liqueur distilled from wine grapes (usually white), it is used as the basis for many sweet-to-dry spirits made with fruits. Cognac and Armagnac are two of the finest aged brandies available.

BREAD

naan the rather thick, leavened bread associated with the tandoori dishes of northern India, where it is baked pressed against the inside wall of a heated tandoor (clay oven). Sold in most supermarkets.

pitta also known as lebanese bread. This wheat-flour pocket bread is sold in large, flat pieces that separate into two thin rounds. Also available in small thick pieces called pocket pitta.

sourdough so-named, not because it's sour in taste, but because it's made by using a small amount of 'starter dough', which contains a yeast culture, mixed into flour and water. Part of the resulting dough is then saved to use as the starter dough next time.

tortilla thin, round unleavened bread; can be made at home or purchased frozen, fresh or vacuum-packed. Two kinds are available, one made from wheat flour and the other from corn.

BROCCOLINI a cross between broccoli and chinese kale; long asparagus-like stems with a long loose floret, both completely edible. Resembles broccoli but is milder and sweeter in taste.

BUK CHOY also known as bok choy, pak choi, Chinese white cabbage or Chinese chard; has a fresh, mild mustard taste. Use stems and leaves, stir-fried or braised. Baby buk choy, also known as pak kat farang or shanghai bok choy, is much smaller and more tender. Its mildly acrid, distinctively appealing taste has made it one of the most commonly used asian greens.

CAPSICUM (BELL PEPPER) also called pepper. Comes in many colours: red, green, yellow, orange and purplish-black. Be sure to discard seeds and membranes before use.

CHEESE

cheddar the most common cow's milk 'tasty' cheese; should be aged, hard and have a pronounced bite.

cream commonly called philadelphia or philly; a soft cow's milk cheese, its fat content ranges from 14 to 33%.

fetta Greek in origin; a crumbly textured goat's or sheep's milk cheese with a sharp, salty taste. Ripened and stored in salted whey; particularly good cubed and tossed into salads.

fetta, persian a soft, creamy fetta marinated in a blend of olive oil, garlic, herbs and spices; available from most major supermarkets.

mozzarella soft, spun-curd cheese originating in southern Italy where it was traditionally made from water-buffalo milk. Now generally made from cow's milk, it is the most popular pizza cheese because of its low melting point and elasticity when heated.

parmesan also called parmigiano; is a hard, grainy cow's milk cheese originating in the Parma region of Italy.

pizza cheese a commercial blend of varying proportions of processed grated mozzarella, cheddar and parmesan.

CHICKEN

drumsticks leg with skin and bone intact.

maryland leg and thigh still connected in a single piece; bones and skin intact.

thigh cutlets thigh with skin and centre bone intact; sometimes found skinned with bone intact.

thigh fillets skin and bone removed.

CHICKPEAS (GARBANZO BEANS)

also called hummus or channa; an irregularly round, sandy-coloured legume used extensively in Mediterranean, Indian and Hispanic cooking. Firm texture even after cooking, a floury mouth-feel and robust nutty flavour; available canned or dried.

CHILLI

chipotle (pronounced cheh-pote-lay) the name used for jalapeño chillies once they've been dried and smoked. Having a deep, intensely smoky flavour, rather than a searing heat, chipotles are dark brown, almost black in colour and wrinkled in appearance.

green any unripened chilli; also some particular varieties that are ripe when green, such as jalapeño, habanero, poblano or serrano.

long red available both fresh and dried; a generic term used for any moderately hot, long, thin chilli (about 6cm to 8cm long).

CHINESE COOKING WINE

also called shao hsing or chinese rice wine; made from fermented rice, wheat, sugar and salt with a 13.5% alcohol content. Inexpensive and found in Asian food shops; if you can't find it, replace with mirin or sherry.

CHINESE FIVE SPICE (FIVE-SPICE POWDER)

a fragrant mixture of ground cinnamon, cloves, star anise, sichuan pepper and fennel seeds.

CHOCOLATE, DARK (SEMI-SWEET)

also called luxury chocolate; made of a high percentage of cocoa liquor and cocoa butter, and little added sugar. Unless stated otherwise, we use dark chocolate in this book as it's ideal for use in desserts and cakes.

CINNAMON

available both in the piece (called sticks or quills) and ground into powder; one of the world's most common spices, used universally as a sweet, fragrant flavouring for both sweet and savoury foods.

COCONUT

cream obtained commercially from the first pressing of the coconut flesh alone, without the addition of water; the second pressing (less rich) is sold as coconut milk. Available in cans and cartons at most supermarkets.

milk not the liquid found inside the fruit (coconut water), but the diluted liquid from the second pressing of the white flesh of a mature coconut (the first pressing produces coconut cream). Available in cans and cartons at most supermarkets.

water is the liquid from the centre of a young green coconut. It has fewer kilojoules than fruit juice, with no fat or protein. There are sugars present, but these are slowly absorbed, giving coconut water a low GI.

CORIANDER (CILANTRO)

also called pak chee or chinese parsley; bright-green-leafed herb with a pungent flavour. The leaves, stems and roots of coriander are also used. Also available ground or as seeds; these should not be substituted for fresh coriander as the tastes are completely different.

CORNFLOUR (CORNSTARCH)

available made from corn or wheat (wheaten cornflour gives a lighter texture in cakes); used as a thickening agent in cooking.

COUSCOUS

a fine, dehydrated, grain-like cereal product made from semolina; it swells to three or four times its original size when liquid is added. It is eaten like rice with a tagine, as a side dish or salad ingredient.

CREAM, POURING

also called pure or fresh cream. It has no additives and contains a minimum fat content of 35%.

CRÈME FRAÎCHE

a mature, naturally fermented cream (minimum fat content 35%) with a velvety texture and slightly tangy, nutty flavour.

CUMIN

also known as zeera or comino; resembling caraway in size, cumin is the dried seed of a plant related to the parsley family.

CURRY PASTES

Some recipes in this book call for commercially prepared pastes of varying strengths and flavours. Use whichever one you feel best suits your spice-level tolerance.

korma a mix of mostly heat-free spices; forms the base of a mild, slightly nutty-tasting, slow-cooked curry.

massaman has a rich, spicy flavour reminiscent of Middle Eastern cooking; favoured by southern Thai cooks for use in hot and sour stew-like curries and satay sauces.

vindaloo a Goan combination of vinegar, tomatoes, pepper and other spices that exemplifies the Portuguese influence on that part of India's coast.

DILL

also called dill weed; used fresh or dried, in seed form or ground. Its anise/celery sweetness flavours the food of the Scandinavian countries, and Germany and Greece. Its feathery, frond-like fresh leaves are grassier and more subtle than the dried version or the seeds (which slightly resemble caraway in flavour).

DUKKAH

an Egyptian specialty spice mixture made up of roasted nuts, seeds and an array of aromatic spices.

EGGPLANT

also known as aubergine. Ranging in size from tiny to very large and in colour from pale green to deep purple. Can also be purchased chargrilled, packed in oil, in jars.

FENNEL also called finocchio or anise; a crunchy green vegetable slightly resembling celery that's eaten raw in salads; fried as an accompaniment; or used as an ingredient in soups and sauces. Also the name given to the dried seeds of the plant which have a stronger licorice flavour.

FLOUR

plain (all-purpose) unbleached wheat flour, the best for baking: the gluten content ensures a strong dough, for a light result.

self-raising all-purpose plain or wholemeal flour with baking powder and salt added; make at home in the proportion of 1 cup plain or wholemeal flour to 2 teaspoons baking powder.

FREEKEH is cracked roasted green wheat and can be found in some larger supermarkets, health food and specialty food stores.

GARAM MASALA a blend of spices including cardamom, cinnamon, cloves, coriander, fennel and cumin, roasted and ground together.

GINGER, FRESH also called green or root ginger; the thick gnarled root of a tropical plant.

HARISSA a Moroccan sauce or paste that's made from dried chillies, cumin, garlic, oil and caraway seeds. The paste, available in a tube, is extremely hot and should not be used in large amounts; bottled harissa sauce is more mild. Available from Middle Eastern food shops and some supermarkets.

KAFFIR LIME LEAVES also known as bai magrood and looks like two glossy dark green leaves joined end to end, forming a rounded hourglass shape. Used fresh or dried in many South-East Asian dishes, they are used like bay leaves or curry leaves, especially in Thai cooking. Sold fresh, dried or frozen, the dried leaves are less potent so double the number if using them as a substitute for fresh; a strip of fresh lime peel may be substituted for each kaffir lime leaf.

LAMB

forequarter chops cut from the shoulder.

sausage, merguez small, spicy sausage believed to have originated in Tunisia but eaten in North Africa, France and Spain; traditionally made with lamb and easily recognised because of its chilli-red colour. Can be fried, grilled or roasted; available from many butchers, delis and specialty sausage stores.

shank forequarter leg; sometimes sold as drumsticks or frenched shanks if the gristle and narrow end of the bone are discarded and the remaining meat trimmed.

shoulder large, tasty piece having much connective tissue so is best pot-roasted or braised. Makes the best mince.

LEEK a member of the onion family, the leek resembles a green onion but is much larger and more subtle in flavour.

LENTILS (RED, BROWN, YELLOW) dried pulses. Eaten by cultures all over the world, most famously perhaps in the dhals of India, lentils have high food value.

French-style green lentils related to the famous French lentils du puy; these green-blue, tiny lentils have a nutty, earthy flavour and a hardy nature, allowing them to be rapidly cooked without disintegrating.

MACADAMIAS native to Australia; fairly large, slightly soft, buttery rich nut. Should always be stored in the fridge to prevent their high oil content turning them rancid.

MAYONNAISE commercial mayonnaise of high quality made with whole eggs and labelled as such; some prepared mayonnaises substitute emulsifiers such as food starch, cellulose gel or other thickeners to mimic the same thick and creamy consistency but never achieve the same rich flavour. Must be refrigerated once opened.

MINT the most commonly used variety of mint is spearmint; it has pointed, bright-green leaves and a fresh flavour.

MIXED SPICE a classic spice mixture generally containing caraway, allspice, coriander, cumin, nutmeg and ginger, although cinnamon and other spices can be added. It is used with fruit and in cakes.

MUSHROOMS, BUTTON small, cultivated white mushrooms with a mild flavour.

MUSTARD

dijon pale brown, distinctively flavoured, fairly mild-tasting French mustard.

wholegrain also known as seeded. A French-style coarse-grain mustard made from crushed mustard seeds and Dijon-style French mustard.

NOODLES

dried rice also called rice stick noodles. Made from rice flour and water, available flat and wide or very thin (vermicelli). Must be soaked in boiling water to soften.

rice stick also called sen lek, ho fun or kway teow; especially popular South-East Asian dried rice noodles. They come in different widths (thin used in soups, wide in stir-fries), but all should be soaked in hot water to soften. The traditional noodle used in pad thai which, before soaking, measures about 5mm in width.

rice vermicelli also called sen mee, mei fun or bee hoon. Used throughout Asia in spring rolls and cold salads; similar to bean threads, only longer and made with rice flour instead of mung bean starch. Before using, soak the dried noodles in hot water until softened, boil them briefly then rinse with hot water.

OIL

olive made from ripened olives. Extra virgin and virgin are the first and second press, respectively, of the olives and are therefore considered the best; 'light' refers to taste not fat levels.

peanut pressed from ground peanuts; most commonly used oil in Asian cooking because of its high smoke point (capacity to handle high heat without burning).

sesame made from roasted, crushed, white sesame seeds; a flavouring rather than a cooking medium.

vegetable oils sourced from plant rather than animal fats.

OLIVES

black have a richer and more mellow flavour than the green ones and are softer in texture. Sold either plain or in a piquant marinade.

green those harvested before fully ripened and are, as a rule, denser and more bitter than the black variety.

ONIONS

brown and white interchangeable; white onions have a more pungent flesh.

green (scallions) also called, incorrectly, shallot; an immature onion picked before the bulb has formed, has a long, bright-green edible stalk.

red also known as spanish, red spanish or bermuda onion; a sweet-flavoured, large, purple-red onion.

shallot also called french or golden shallots or eschalots; small and elongated with a brown skin.

ORANGE SWEET POTATO also known as kumara. Often confused with yam.

OREGANO a herb, also known as wild marjoram; has a woody stalk and clumps of tiny, dark-green leaves. Has a pungent, peppery flavour.

PAPRIKA ground, dried, sweet red capsicum (bell pepper); there are many grades and types available, including sweet, hot, mild and smoked.

PARSLEY a versatile herb with a fresh, earthy flavour. There are about 30 varieties of curly parsley; the flat-leaf variety (also called continental or italian parsley) is stronger in flavour and darker in colour.

PARSNIP a root vegetable closely related to carrot and parsley; can be baked, mashed or made into chips.

PASTA

macaroni tube-shaped pasta available in various sizes; made from semolina and water; does not contain eggs.

spaghetti long, thin solid strands of pasta.

spiral corkscrew-shaped pasta available in various flavours and sizes.

PEAS

green also known as garden peas; must be shelled and their pods never eaten. Peas in the pod will yield just under half their weight of shelled peas; 1kg (2lb) will serve 4. Peas in the pod are available fresh and shelled peas are available frozen.

snow also called mangetout; a variety of garden pea, eaten pod and all (although you may need to string them). Used in stir-fries or eaten raw in salads. Snow pea sprouts are available from supermarkets or greengrocers and are usually eaten raw in salads or sandwiches.

sugar snap also called honey snap peas; fresh small pea which can be eaten, whole, pod and all, similarly to snow peas.

PECANS native to the US and now grown locally; pecans are golden brown, buttery and rich. Good in savoury as well as sweet dishes; walnuts are a good substitute.

PEPPERCORNS, BLACK picked when the berry is not quite ripe, then dried until it shrivels and the skin turns dark brown/black. It's the strongest flavoured of the three (white, green and black) – slightly hot with a hint of sweetness.

PINE NUTS also known as pignoli; not a nut but a small, cream-coloured kernel from pine cones. They are best roasted before use to bring out the flavour.

PISTACHIOS green, delicately flavoured nuts inside hard off-white shells. Available salted or unsalted in their shells; you can also buy them shelled. We use the weight of shelled nuts in our recipes.

POLENTA also known as cornmeal; a ground, flour-like cereal made of dried corn (maize) sold in several different textures. Also the name of the dish made from it.

POMEGRANATE dark-red, leathery-skinned fresh fruit about the size of an orange filled with hundreds of seeds, each wrapped in an edible lucent-crimson pulp having a unique tangy sweet-sour flavour.

molasses not to be confused with pomegranate syrup or grenadine; pomegranate molasses is thicker, browner, and more concentrated in flavour – tart and sharp, slightly sweet and fruity.

PORK

American-style spare ribs usually sold in long slabs or racks of 10 to 12 ribs, trimmed so little fat remains; slather with barbecue sauce before cooking.

ham hock the lower portion of the leg; includes the meat, fat and bone. Most have been cured, smoked or both, but fresh hocks are sometimes available.

minced ground lean pork.

prosciutto a kind of unsmoked Italian ham; salted, air-cured and aged, it is usually eaten uncooked.

sausage, chorizo of Spanish origin, made from coarsely minced (ground) smoked pork and highly seasoned with garlic, chilli powder and other spices.

sausage, italian pork available as both sweet, which is flavoured with garlic and fennel seeds, and hot, which has chilli added.

speck smoked pork.

shoulder joint sold with bone in or out.

QUINCE yellow-skinned fruit with hard texture and astringent, tart taste; eaten cooked or as a preserve. Long, slow cooking makes the flesh a deep rose pink.

quince paste a thick quince preserve which is sliceable; served on a cheese platter; goes well with cheeses such as brie and camembert. Available from most supermarkets and delicatessens.

RICE

basmati a white, fragrant long grain rice; the grains fluff up when cooked. Wash several times before cooking.

brown retains the high-fibre, nutritious bran coating that's removed from white rice when hulled. It takes longer to cook than white rice and has a chewier texture. Once cooked, the long grains stay separate, while the short grains are soft and stickier.

jasmine a long grain white rice recognised around the world as having a perfumed aromatic quality; moist in texture, it clings together after cooking. Sometimes substituted for basmati rice.

ROCKET (ARUGULA) also called rugula and rucola; peppery green leaf eaten raw in salads or used in cooking. Baby rocket leaves are smaller and less peppery.

ROSEMARY pungent herb with long, thin pointy leaves; use large and small sprigs, and finely chop leaves.

SAFFRON stigma of a member of the crocus family, available ground or in strands; imparts a yellow-orange colour to food once infused. The quality can vary greatly; the best is the most expensive spice in the world. Should be stored in the freezer.

SAGE pungent herb with narrow, grey-green leaves; slightly bitter with a slightly musty mint aroma. Refrigerate fresh sage wrapped in paper towel and sealed in a plastic bag for up to 4 days. Dried sage comes whole, crumbled or ground. It should be stored in a cool, dark place for no more than three months.

SAUCES

char siu a Chinese barbecue sauce made from sugar, water, salt, fermented soybean paste, honey, soy sauce, malt syrup and spices. Found at most supermarkets.

fish also called nam pla or nuoc nam; made from pulverised salted fermented fish, most often anchovies. Has a very pungent smell and strong taste, so use according to your taste level.

hoisin barbecue sauce made from salted fermented soybeans, onions and garlic; used as a marinade or baste, or to accentuate stir-fries and barbecued or roasted foods. Available from Asian food shops and supermarkets.

kecap manis a thick, dark, salty Indonesian soy sauce.

oyster Asian in origin, this rich, brown sauce is made from oysters and their brine, cooked with salt and soy sauce, and thickened with starches.

soy also known as sieu; made from fermented soybeans. Several variations are available in most supermarkets and Asian food stores. We use a mild Japanese variety in our recipes.

sriracha is a medium-hot chilli sauce available from Asian food stores and some major supermarkets.

sweet chilli comparatively mild, fairly sticky and runny bottled sauce made from red chillies, sugar, garlic and white vinegar; used in Thai cooking.

SHORTCRUST PASTRY, READY-ROLLED packaged sheets of frozen shortcrust pastry, available from supermarkets.

SILVER BEET (SWISS CHARD) also called, incorrectly, spinach; has fleshy stalks and large leaves and can be prepared as for spinach.

SPINACH also called english spinach and incorrectly, silver beet. Baby spinach leaves are best eaten raw in salads; the larger leaves should be added last to soups, stews and stir-fries, and should be cooked until barely wilted.

STAR ANISE dried star-shaped pod with an astringent aniseed flavour; used to flavour stocks and marinades. Available whole and ground, it is an essential ingredient in five-spice powder.

SUGAR

caster (superfine) finely granulated table sugar.

brown a soft, finely granulated sugar retaining molasses for its characteristic colour and flavour.

TAHINI a rich, sesame-seed paste.

TARRAGON french tarragon, with its subtle aniseed flavour, complements chicken, eggs and veal, and is perfect in a béarnaise sauce. It is also one of the herbs that make up the French fines herbs. Russian and Mexican tarragons are slightly coarser in taste.

THYME a member of the mint family, it has tiny grey-green leaves that give off a pungent minty, light-lemon aroma. Dried thyme comes in both leaf and powder form.

TOMATOES

bottled pasta sauce a prepared sauce; a blend of tomatoes, herbs and spices.

canned whole peeled tomatoes in natural juices; available crushed, chopped or diced. Use undrained.

cherry also called tiny tim or tom thumb tomatoes; small and round.

passata sieved tomato puree. To substitute, puree and sieve canned tomatoes or use canned tomato puree which is similar, but slightly thicker.

paste triple-concentrated tomato puree used to flavour soups, stews and sauces.

puree canned pureed tomatoes.

truss small vine-ripened tomatoes with vine still attached.

TREACLE thick, dark syrup not unlike molasses; a by-product of the sugar refining process.

VINEGAR

balsamic originally from Modena, Italy, there are now many balsamic vinegars on the market ranging in pungency and quality depending on how, and for how long, they have been aged. Made from the juice of trebbiano grapes; it is a deep rich brown colour with a sweet and sour flavour. Quality can be determined up to a point by price; use the most expensive sparingly.

cider (apple cider) made from crushed fermented apples.

rice a colourless vinegar made from fermented rice and flavoured with sugar and salt. Sherry can be substituted.

wine made from a blend of either white or red wines.

WOMBOK (NAPA CABBAGE) also called chinese cabbage or peking cabbage; elongated in shape with pale green, crinkly leaves. The most common cabbage in South-East Asia. Can be shredded or chopped and eaten raw or braised, steamed or stir-fried.

YOGHURT, GREEK-STYLE often made from sheep's milk that is strained in a cloth (traditionally muslin) to remove the whey and to give it a thick, smooth, creamy consistency, almost like whipped cream.

ZA'ATAR a Middle Eastern herb and spice mixture which varies but always includes thyme and ground sumac and, usually, toasted sesame seeds. It is sprinkled on yoghurt and flatbreads and can be used as a rub on lamb or chicken when grilled or roasted.

ZUCCHINI also known as courgette; small green, yellow or white vegetable belonging to the squash family. When harvested young, its edible flowers can be stuffed, then deep-fried or oven-baked.

Conversion chart

MEASURES

One Australian metric measuring cup holds approximately 250ml; one Australian metric tablespoon holds 20ml; one Australian metric teaspoon holds 5ml. The difference between one country's measuring cups and another's is within a two- or three-teaspoon variance and will not affect your cooking results. North America, New Zealand and the United Kingdom use a 15ml tablespoon. All cup and spoon measurements are level.

The most accurate way of measuring dry ingredients is to weigh them.

When measuring liquids, use a clear glass or plastic jug with the metric markings.

We use large eggs with an average weight of 60g.

DRY MEASURES

metric	imperial
15g	½oz
30g	1oz
60g	2oz
90g	3oz
125g	4oz (¼lb)
155g	5oz
185g	6oz
220g	7oz
250g	8oz (½lb)
280g	9oz
315g	10oz
345g	11oz
375g	12oz (¾lb)
410g	13oz
440g	14oz
470g	15oz
500g	16oz (1lb)
750g	24oz (1½lb)
1kg	32oz (2lb)

LIQUID MEASURES

metric	imperial
30ml	1 fluid oz
60ml	2 fluid oz
100ml	3 fluid oz
125ml	4 fluid oz
150ml	5 fluid oz
190ml	6 fluid oz
250ml	8 fluid oz
300ml	10 fluid oz
500ml	16 fluid oz
600ml	20 fluid oz
1000ml (1 litre)	1¾ pints

LENGTH MEASURES

metric	imperial
3mm	⅛in
6mm	¼in
1cm	½in
2cm	¾in
2.5cm	1in
5cm	2in
6cm	2½in
8cm	3in
10cm	4in
13cm	5in
15cm	6in
18cm	7in
20cm	8in
22cm	9in
25cm	10in
28cm	11in
30cm	12in (1ft)

OVEN TEMPERATURES

The oven temperatures in this book are for conventional ovens; if you have a fan-forced oven, decrease the temperature by 10–20 degrees.

	°C (Celsius)	°F (Fahrenheit)
Very slow	120	250
Slow	150	300
Moderately slow	160	325
Moderate	180	350
Moderately hot	200	400
Hot	220	425
Very hot	240	475

Index

W

Y

R